As If People Mattered
Dignity in Organizations

By
Bernard H. Baum

authorHOUSE™
1663 Liberty Drive, Suite 200
Bloomington, Indiana 47403
(800) 839-8640
www.AuthorHouse.com

This book is a work of non-fiction. Unless otherwise noted, the author and the publisher make no explicit guarantees as to the accuracy of the information contained in this book and in some cases, names of people and places have been altered to protect their privacy.

First published by AuthorHouse 08/30/05

ISBN: 1-4208-2308-6 (sc)
ISBN: 1-4208-2307-8 (dj)

Library of Congress Control Number: 2005907983

Printed in the United States of America
Bloomington, Indiana

This book is printed on acid-free paper.

FOR BARBARA, IN MEMORY

Table of Contents

Chapter Four

Chapter Five

Chapter Six

Chapter Seven

Preface

As a student of organizational behavior, I began my career with a study of the delegation of authority. I quickly learned that many recipients perceived this merely as the delegation of extra work. In a subsequent study regarding employee perceptions of the discrepancy between their actual influence and desired influence, control per se did not emerge as the primary concern. What mattered more to employees was that any delegation of authority should be matched by a greater degree of management-acknowledged dignity. Efforts by management to improve the organizational climate and culture were generally perceived by employees not only as disingenuous attempts to get them to work harder, but also as insults to their intelligence and further denigration of their dignity. That early observation had a major impact on my subsequent research. I focused my attention on the nature and distribution of authority, influence, and control. In recent years, I have come to realize that two widely held perceptions—that employee "empowerment" is a disguise for harder work, and that authority is persistently abused—share an underlying commonality: the erosion of dignity.

My review of pertinent literature showed that dignity is an understudied concept in organizational research, generally relegated to the academic discourses of theology and philosophy. The term itself is often associated with old ways and mores. Responding to the notion that dignity was a relatively neglected area of study, a colleague commented, "That's because dignity is like chivalry—it's passed off the scene." (A year later, at a large national meeting, the same colleague would advocate the use of dignity as a marketing concept.)

The denigration of dignity within the organizational context is most often viewed as a labor issue. Experts in the field of labor studies can testify to the importance of countering systematic denigration as a driving force behind the establishment of trade unions. However, because dignity is such an intangible concept, labor scholars have tended to focus more on such quantifiable factors as wages, hours, and working conditions. After years of studying organization behavior and culture, I have come to the conclusion that dignity is a basic human need that must be taken into account in any analysis of management strategy and employee relations. The concept of dignity sheds light on many of the most salient questions of organizational sociology, especially concerning the nature and distribution of authority, influence, and control.

Although large organizations are no longer viewed as quasi-permanent employers, workplace dignity remains a crucial issue for workers and for society. The modern organization has become the ultimate social bonding agent, to a large extent supplanting smaller-scale groupings, such as extended families, neighborhoods, and religious affiliations. As communal ties weaken, the workplace becomes the central arena in the struggle for a humane and meaningful life.

There is some urgency to this view, as technology threatens to further dehumanize the workplace. Halls of electronic workstations have become the new sweatshops, where Big Brother can keep an eye on every electronic move we make. We are both isolated and controlled, and the interpersonal relationships that are at the heart of dignity are neglected.

What is dignity? Over the course of my research, I have come to think in terms of a process that I call *dignifying*. In our interpersonal contacts, we dignify or denigrate one another. By positing these two terms as the poles of a spectrum of behaviors, we can map workplace attitudes and practices and understand their effect on people. Mutual respect and honest two-way communication are mechanisms which create dignity. Intimidation, humiliation, and degradation are prime examples of denigrating behavior that, in the long term, saps morale and productivity. They are obstacles to team building and knowledge sharing. Promoting dignity means eradicating the latter behaviors and fostering dignifying behaviors in their place.

This book is the result of many interviews with employees and discussions with a wide variety of colleagues, from which emerged a theory of dignity, dignifying, and denigration. This presentation is heavy on example and anecdote, as befits a topic that is both highly subjective and culturally relative. The case histories show how the presence or absence of dignifying attitudes and actions often spells the difference between success and failure in organizational initiatives.

In this brief book, I have attempted to address the complex question of dignity at both the macro and micro level. The dignity of the individual is a critical issue for any society. Actions that dignify or denigrate are rooted in choices made by human beings who operate within organizational contexts. Integrating dignity into corporate strategy and cultures is the task at hand. A corporate culture that has integrated dignity will optimally nurture human potential and thus be optimally productive.

Bernard H. Baum

Acknowledgements

This book would not have been possible without the help of many people who assisted me every step of the way. Chief among these was Christopher Morrsink, Ph.D., who provided me with constructive editing of our mutually developed ideas, e.g. the concept of "dignifying." This work represents a joint venture of Dr. Morrsink and me.

I am grateful for the editing work of Hugh Iglarsh and Daniel London. My daughter, Lisa Kritz, did a wonderful job of providing insightful constructive criticism.

Gwendolyn Slaughter provided conscientious transcribing and typing services.

My appreciation extends to all the unidentified persons whose responses constitute the heart of this work.

Introduction: Dignity in Organizations

Human dignity is more than just an abstract principle. From an organizational perspective, it is a variable of great importance for managers, workers, clients, and policy-makers. Central to this book is the argument that workers and managers who are committed to dignifying others contribute to a positive work climate and are the most successful in the long run. Yet, dignity and dignifying are seldom-used terms in the field of organizational theory. Even when used in the title of a book or chapter, they are often not elaborated upon at all.[1] The lack of attention is due in part to sociologists' tendency to focus on quantitative measures, and to reduced interest among decision-makers in the human costs of an increasingly deregulated economic system.

In light of rising workplace violence and stress, however, the business world has slowly begun to realize that it ignores human dignity at its own peril. Many business schools are refocusing their curricula around the ethics of decision-making, and some corporations are addressing and showing renewed interest in issues of social responsibility, including arts, education, and healthcare. This book goes beyond the tokenism of most corporate standards of community involvement to argue that a permanent focus on human dignity in decision-making improves the quality of the work experience from the perspective of employees and enhances organizational effectiveness.

The Uses of "Dignity"

The goal of creating and maintaining a culture of decency, in which the dignity of each individual is recognized, has great appeal.[2] Many published works discuss the topics of illness and dying within the framework of patient dignity. The gay rights movement has based its drive for equality around this concept, often breaking taboos in

---

1 See, for example, Chapter 5: "Working Conditions: Health and Safety, Dignity and Autonomy on the Job," in *Solutions for the New Work Force: Policies for a new social contract*, eds. John J. Sweeney and Karen Nussbaum. (Washington, D.C.: Seven Locks Press, 1989).

2 We borrow the term "culture of decency" from Dr. Shaheer H. Khan of the Aligarh Muslim University in India.

the process.[3] Among workers, the cry for dignity has been a rallying force for centuries. Recently, workers in England have begun a campaign for a Dignity at Work Act, mostly to counteract the bullying tendencies of supervisors and management.[4] Dignity has become a contagious word in the commercial sector, used for everything from funeral parlors and nursing homes to pension funds.

Hundreds of published works contain the word *dignity.* Most fit into one of four categories: dignity in healthcare and dying; gay, lesbian, bisexual, and transgender rights; rights of the mentally and physically disabled; and dignity for the poor and the underprivileged. Also, many texts approach dignity from a theological or purely ethical perspective. Very rare are books and articles that address human dignity in an organizational context. Although there is an extensive literature about the dehumanizing aspects of work, workers are more often conceptualized as human capital than as human beings. A sterling—and somewhat lonely—example of a dignifying corporate leader was the chief executive officer of a burned-down textile plant in Massachusetts who, knowing that employees are the organization, kept all workers on the payroll until the mill could be rebuilt. More typical, unfortunately, are the actions of Chiquita Brands International in Honduras after the devastating Hurricane Mitch of October 1998. All 7,400 Honduran workers, whose wages constituted a miniscule portion of the Chiquita budget, were laid off. Insult was added to injury.

The term *dignity* is often used in trade union literature and the political platforms of European social-democratic parties. Dignity serves as a rallying cry for social movements and social action. From these perspectives, *dignity of work* is viewed as a counterforce to the forces of mass production. The goal of preserving human dignity, in this sense, underlies much of our labor relations legislation. The

---

3 An example of such taboo breaking is DignityUSA, Inc., an organization devoted to expanding the rights of gay, lesbian, bisexual, and transgender Catholics within the Church.

4 Amicus-MSF Union, "Parliament Debates Workplace Bullying," <http://www.amicustheunion.org/main.asp?page=344> (accessed March 16, 2005).

worldview and rhetoric of union leaders is grounded in the principle that each worker has dignity.

But very little literature deals with dignity from a managerial or organizational perspective. Our task is to present dignity as an organizational goal that can be incorporated into the management strategies of modern business.

Dignity in a Post-Modern World

The Chinese curse, "May you live in interesting times," captures the ambivalence that many of us experience in assessing our present period and prospects. We *do* live in interesting times, and not always for the better. Technological developments, population growth, massive migration, and economic globalization are driving us into new social and political territory. Social changes take place at breakneck speed, often challenging our worldviews. Many social barriers to economic achievement have eroded or disappeared. Ecumenical activities in churches have become almost routine, bringing together denominations that not long ago were engaged in ideological or even physical confrontation. In the U.S. presidential election of 1960, Senator John F. Kennedy's Catholicism was a major issue. A quarter of a century later, the Pope himself became a celebrity in the United States, largely in light of his association with the collapse of Communism in Eastern Europe. At the same time, the Internet, cable television, and underground radio have provided nongovernmental organizations and social movements of every stripe, including terrorist organizations and hate groups that attempt to dehumanize whole populations, with cheap and easy means to broadcast their messages electronically to global audiences.

Social science concepts such as the liquid society, virtual reality, chaos theory, and social relativism try to capture the essence and relevance of these broad global developments. Journalist David Standish comments on how members in society are coping with the uncertainty and stress of modern times. Governmental bureaucracies and politicians struggling to find adequate responses to growing social problems have frequently turned to Machiavellian solutions, from chain gangs and 50,000-volt stun belts for controlling convicts, to the building of massive prisons. Standish blames computers and technology for the loneliness that people experience, which is transformed into a meanness that camouflages our vulnerability in weakened social settings.[5]

Belief in unlimited progress and growth, translated into higher wages and increased consumption, is at the core of the modernity paradigm. Organizations are measured by their profitability and their potential growth. Human beings are measured, and often measure themselves, by their bank accounts, income, houses, job skills, and educational degrees. This emphasis on quantifiable measures of achievement has long troubled organizational theorists and ethicists, who see it as fundamentally dehumanizing and destructive of our sense of wholeness. The latter cannot be attained, they have repeatedly asserted, in a Marxist fashion, by abolishing private ownership of the means of production. Rather, it can be achieved only by working within existing economic frameworks to create work environments that encourage mutually dignifying interactions among people at all levels of an organization.

The problem of organizing work in the late-modern era lies in the perceived tension between efficiency, which involves division of labor, and human dignity, which sees workers as a whole. Taking its inspiration from the works of non-Marxist organizational theorists, this book seeks to explore the consequences of either denigrating or enhancing human dignity in the workplace, and to examine the options available to management, trade unions, and policy-makers

---

5 David Standish, "The Age of Mean: It's Terrible Out There, But is it Worse Than Ever?" *Chicago Tribune*, June 22, 1997, p.12. These matters have also been the subject of lengthy discussion in scholarly works. Kiel (1994) explores the managerial use of chaos theory, with its search for the deep structure within. Giddens (1991) describes the conditions of late modernity, focusing on contradictions embodied in social practices. Charles Handy encapsulates our era as *The Age of Paradox* (1994). However, these paradoxes and contradictions often stay hidden in our subconscious. Marsden and Townley (1996), describing the worldview behind most organizational theories, capture this ambiguous quality of post-modern existence: "Modernity is Janus-faced: it enriches and impoverishes, empowers and represses, organizes life within the workplace and atomizes life in civil society on the streets and in the homes, enhances efficiency and dehumanizes."

who seek to humanize the workplace by balancing organizational goals with the needs of individuals.

The focus on dignity in the organization means that this book must bypass thought-provoking discussions in the fields of healthcare ethics, politics, religion, and philosophy. Our goal is to demonstrate that dignity is a topic worthy of the attention of organizational decision-makers, and that by creating and maintaining a dignifying climate, organizations can better fulfill their mission. To that end the book is divided into three sections. The first part is a theoretical discussion of the concept of dignity, an analysis of the concept in light of current organizational principles and theories, and suggestions as to how dignity can be integrated into managerial strategy. In Chapter Two, we show that the lack of dignity in modern management thinking is grounded in certain structural and cultural forces. In Chapter Three, we address these cultural forces from the employee's perspective.

The second section of the book presents a series of examples of the social, personal, and economic costs associated with denigrating behavior (Chapter Four), as well as dignifying strategies to counter these behaviors (Chapter Five). Each chapter provides descriptive examples of dignity within the work setting, as well as in the interaction between organizations and the public.

The third and concluding section offers ways to develop management programs aimed at promoting dignity and preventing denigration. Chapter Six addresses the need for self-reflection and uses the stage theory of behavioral/attitudinal change to suggest steps that a manager can take to prepare for a dignifying work role. In Chapter Seven, we deal with the group dynamics and contextual realities of all organizations as open systems. Relying strongly on a contingency approach to positive change, we present a series of suggestions and caveats, from which readers can find their own unique pathways.

###

Chapter One

A Brief History:
From Feudal Dignity to Democratic Dignity

The concept of dignity has been around for thousands of years. The sacred texts of the world's great religions recognize a God who confers dignity on all human beings. Yet, today we think about dignity primarily in social terms, as something produced by relationships between people. Treating dignity as a product of social interactions dates at least to feudal Europe, where dignity was defined as *the quality of being worthy or honorable* as determined by social rank. Feudal rituals gave symbolic weight to this conception. Wearing the mantle of the judiciary, wearing the crown, and the right to bear arms all developed as symbols of dignity. Other professions or positions of high status were likewise recognized by distinct symbols and clothing. Establishing a coat of arms was a dignifying moment for feudal families, clans, and cities, and later, for nation states. In similar fashion, indignity, the state of social unworthiness, was given ritual confirmation by acts such as branding of the flesh or being required to kneel before one's social superiors.

Dignity is still linked to rituals of social stratification in some societies. While shaking hands as a greeting ritual symbolizes an equality of partners, farmers in the Veluwe region of the Netherlands extend more fingers to those of greater social status: one finger is extended to those considered lower in worth, while three fingers are for equals and four (a full hand) shows great respect.

Demotion and promotion in the army, police, and other uniformed services are linked to the number of stripes or stars on the uniform. High status, which commands deferential treatment from subordinates, is referred to as "joining the brass." Modern-day corporations use tokens of dignity and indignity to affirm their hierarchies. One European pharmaceutical company developed a system of coffee drinking incorporating no fewer than eleven ranks. At the lowest level of the hierarchy, workers got coffee in Styrofoam cups. The board of directors enjoyed their coffee in porcelain cups and saucers, using spoons with the company's logo (a modern-day equivalent of the coat of arms). The president's cup and saucer had a golden rim. It may be no coincidence that the company went bankrupt in 1979.[6]

Max Weber, discussing the ideal type of bureaucracy, described social prestige as a variant of this feudal concept of dignity. He referred to the dignitaries in the industrialized, bureaucratized world as the communal, administrative, and professional elites on the top rungs of organizational hierarchies.

Feudalism emphasized the assessment of an individual's social worth in terms of social stratification. Yet social stratification puts a premium on being from the right school, the right family, the right race, or the right religious or ethnic group. It is the feudal equivalence of status and dignity that made it possible to consider serfs the property of lords, wives the property of husbands, and slaves the property of plantation owners. Implicit in the notion of a democratic society is the rejection of these rigid social classifications as a measure of the individual's social value.

The ancient and ongoing practice of attempting to deny the human dignity of specific groups lies at the root of many social upheavals. When the Thracian Gladiator Spartacus led a slave revolt throughout the Roman Republic, he was aided by the widespread denigration experienced by the lowest social strata. In the sixteenth century, the Dutch revolt against the Spanish crown spawned the name *geuzen* ("beggars"), intended by the Spaniards as a term of derision. Instead of being humbled by the label, the Dutch adopted it as a term of pride and still use it today. The appropriation by American militiamen of the derisive British song "Yankee Doodle" tells a similar story of a group of people overcoming attempts to deride their community. Frantz Fanon, Julius Nyerere, Mohandas Gandhi, and other leaders and intellectuals from less developed countries portrayed the resistance against imperialism as a struggle against not only economic exploitation, but also the racist and dehumanizing attitudes of the colonizers.

Racism and caste are among the social structures designed to control the sense of dignity or denigration experienced by members of the race or caste. In the United States, racism and indignity are

---

6 Personal observation.

closely intertwined. As an African-American professor who grew up in segregated Baltimore stated, "If you have black skin, you are always operating at the mercy of the [white] observer in giving you your humanity—and it can always be taken away. This insecurity, which is based on my skin and not my merit, must underlie all my strategic actions."[7]

The old equation of status and social dignity finds its expression in many current ethical questions. The question of which patients should receive organ transplants—that is, who deserves to live—tests our society's concepts of equality and worth. When Pennsylvania governor Robert P. Casey received heart and liver transplants in 1994 just a few weeks after being diagnosed with a rare degenerative condition, many questions were raised about how political clout influenced the medical decision-making process. Similar questions about how we assess worth arise in education, where children of alumni are granted preferential treatment. Behind our much-trumpeted enthusiasm for meritocracy lie vestiges of the feudal concept of human worth and human dignity.

Dignity and Diplomacy

The elaborate protocols that govern trade, diplomacy, and conflict management—even warfare—illustrate the importance of the concept of dignity. The following vignette illustrates the challenges that diplomacy often presents:

> Aboikoni, the elderly *Granman* of the Saramacaner tribe in Suriname, South America, was in a meeting with his secretaries in Djoemoe, planning the reception for Queen Juliana of the Netherlands. An important issue of protocol had to be addressed. One of the male secretaries advised that the seating arrangements should be such that the two monarchs would be at the same height. Another advised, however, that the *kaptynbangis* (ornamental chairs used in these high-status affairs) were meant for men and that they are uncomfortable for women, who normally use the lower *oemabangi*.

7 Personal interview.

Embarrassment had to be avoided. A third secretary argued that no woman had ever been allowed to sit in a *kaptynbangi*, and that this would establish a precedent. How to solve the dilemma?

The secretary closest to Aboikoni suggested a solution. Since Aboikoni was at least thirty years older than Queen Juliana and was, in fact, the oldest royal in the world at that time, it would be all right if he sat on the high chair and the Dutch queen on the low *oemabanji*, if the floor for both were even. Age should be acknowledged. And so it was agreed. The queen and the Granman had a royal conversation, and when the party was over, the queen greeted every functionary and every servant with a handshake and called them by their name. It was a dignifying moment.

Genocide is considered a crime against humanity rather than a justifiable act of war because it consciously denigrates not only individuals, but entire peoples. In the same vein, anger in the United States at the killing of American soldiers in Somalia in 1993 turned to outrage when the soldiers' corpses were mutilated. For many Americans, these actions spoke not only of the tragedy of war, but of the blatant disregard for human dignity that sometimes surfaces in times of war.

> How to supervise and discipline is culturally bound by perceptions of dignity. In Latin America, for example, "*Dignidad* can undermine working hours and foreman control when workers quit their jobs after being reprimanded for lateness, absence, or poor work. The *dignidad de la persona* refers to the inner integrity or worth that every person is supposed to have and guards jealously, and has nothing to do with dignity of social position, office, or role. An allied characteristic of Hispanic culture is *personalismo*—namely the pattern that prescribes for Latin Americans trust only for those persons with whom he or she is in personal relationships. Only such persons can have a reciprocal appreciation of one's soul, and with such individuals one can feel secure." (Harris and Moran, 1987)

For all its importance, dignity is a difficult subject to study because it is a culturally subjective term. In Western societies, people often show respect for others by asking questions about their feelings. Thais show respect for the feelings of others by avoiding asking deeply personal questions. In Thailand, discussing *sagsi* (dignity) may violate rules of decorum and dignity.

Dignity is a powerful issue in minority-majority relationships in society. The sense of second-class citizenship felt by members of many minority groups is based on the perception that their humanity and equality are not fully affirmed and acknowledged by their neighbors. The Chinese in Malaysia share this perception with Koreans in Japan, Catholics in Northern Ireland, African-Americans in the United States, Native Americans in the United States and Canada, indigenous Hawaiians in Hawaii, and Huguenots in early modern France. In the province of Quebec, the French-speaking population argues from the perspective of secondary status, as does the Dutch-speaking community of Belgium. In conflicts such as these, accumulated indignities are an important factor. In some Western societies, governments have gone as far as to make public apologies for historic discrimination and persecution of minority populations. Germany's compensation to victims of the Nazi Holocaust is perhaps the most significant example. However, subsequent examples include U.S. president Bill Clinton's 1997 apology to African-Americans.[8]

In the training centers of multinational corporations, business executives take lessons in the intricacies of dignifying in other cultures. Many students become fluent in the forms of etiquette and behavior, but not in the underlying values and norms.[9] In a diverse work world and a global marketplace, there is increased need for sensitivity to intercultural dignity. Changing our attitude toward dignifying on a global scale can be considered an investment in social capital. What matters is not only whom you know, but how you maintain relationships and bestow dignity in each encounter.

---

8 In Canada, the government recently apologized to its aboriginal peoples for centuries of exploitation and cultural genocide. (See New York Times News Service, "Canada Apologizes to Aboriginal People," *Chicago Tribune*, January 8, 1998.)

9 W.B. Gudykunst, *Bridging Differences: Effective Intergroup Communication* (Newbury Park: Sage Publications, 1991).

Democratic Dignity

Dignity is a variable that cannot be defined outside the sphere of human interaction. One can only have dignity and give dignity in relation to others. We understand dignity as a commitment to regard and treat others, and to be regarded and treated by others, as:

- unique
- fundamentally equal
- an end rather than a means

Defined this way, dignity appears similar to *respect*. However, a show of respect may be precisely that, a show. Respect can be one-way, situational, or conditional.[10] Dignity is deeper, reflecting a fundamental set of beliefs about one's relationships with others. To dignify is to acknowledge the value of every human being. Understanding human beings as persons and not as functions is at the core of the dignifying attitude.

> On April 2, 1994, Secretary-General Kofi Annan refused to "*dignify with a reply*" a remark by a U.S. congressman, who said that Annan "ought to be horsewhipped" for his dealings with Iraqi President Saddam Hussein. (Horsewhipping was the traditional punishment for slaves and other social inferiors.) Workers can highlight denigrating behavior by refusing to respond to it.

Dignity is also connected to self-esteem. In Central America, the term *dignidad* is connected to self-respect, machismo, and honor. Brockner discusses self-esteem as a psychological variable or personality characteristic reflecting a sense of self-worth.[11] In *Self-Esteem at Work*, he illustrates how an employee's self-esteem helps explain his or her workplace behavior. Unlike self-esteem, dignity is a social variable, accorded or denied by others. While denigration and indignity can play a role in undermining self-esteem, the concepts should not be used interchangeably, as self-esteem is essentially a personal and psychological quality while dignity is mutual and cultural.

---

10 Naomi Morris, "Respect: Its meaning and measurement as an element of patient care," *Journal of Public Health Policy* 18 (1997): 133-154.

11 J. Brockner, Self-*esteem at work: Research, theory, and practice* (Lexington, MA: Lexington Books, 1988).

Dignity is an inclusionary and unifying force. When we dignify others, we ourselves are dignified. Dignity satisfies our deep need for belonging and counteracts the forces of alienation. Dignity strengthens our society, expands our circles, and solidifies our networks. Dignity does not preclude competition, but it humanizes its consequences. The Geneva Convention and the concept of war crime are both based on the widely accepted notion that even during war, minimal standards of dignity with respect to the treatment of human beings apply. War may justify violence; it cannot justify indignity.

We can think of dignifying as the essence of inclusive behavior and denigration as it's opposite, exclusionary behavior. When Socrates claimed that dignity must be bestowed on every citizen of Athens, he meant just that. Women did not count, nor did slaves, foreigners, or non-Athenian Greeks. Within these limits, the Socratic notion of dignity was deeply democratic. However, it prevented Socrates—as it does those who today harbor exclusionary attitudes—from recognizing the dignity of all human beings. Those who celebrate diversity can do so only because they embrace the modern idea of universal dignity.

###

Chapter Two

Beyond Marxism

The Centrality of Work

We spend a huge portion of our lives in educational and work environments. From the age of four, or even earlier, we engage in group activities outside the home, sometimes for more than half our waking hours. We are constantly occupied with the task of defining our social roles in relation to others. We give meaning and structure to our lives through school and work. When identifying ourselves to others, we give our names first, then tell what we do and where we do it. Our identities are signified almost as much by our roles as by our names. From an early age, we find our significance in social interaction depending upon others to bestow upon us a sense of self-worth. When we cannot find satisfaction in these interactions, we claim the right to withhold dignity from other participants or withdraw from the relationship.

But we cannot withdraw entirely from society. We have no choice but to associate with others. Nor can we escape the influence of community, school, workplace, and legal system. Beyond our own sense of self-worth and individuality, we seek validation in organizational structures where power is unevenly distributed. Marx was correct to point out that we learn to accept the lowest common denominator of human worth, a wage or commission, as a way to earn a living and get ahead in a competitive society. Yet Marx was too quick to pin the blame for the ennui he perceived among the working classes on the worker's alienation from the product of his or her labors. He refused to consider the possibility that the tribulations of the working class could be addressed in large part by addressing the characteristics of relations between management and workers. In short, he did not confront the possibility that the quality of relations between people was at the heart of the problem for the workers of nineteenth century Europe, not the quality of relations between workers and the goods they produced.

Whether, as Marx asserted, human beings yearn for an enduring connection with the goods they produce, is a question this book will not address. Regardless of the conclusion of that debate, there is one human yearning of which we can be certain. Human beings seek fulfillment through relations with others, through recognition from all of those with whom they come in contact. A family story passed on from one generation to the next illustrates this need:

> Grandpa Morrsink was proud of the gold watch and plaque he got for fifty-three years of loyal and reliable service to the textile company where he started working as a twelve-year-old. From the outside, it may seem that he was exploited by the company, but for him, the company was the core of his life. His peers and his bosses liked him and visited him at home far into his retirement. He remembered with satisfaction the camaraderie, the occasional strike, the introduction of new machinery and new knowledge. However exploitative his work life might seem to us today, we could never deny him his right to view his life and work from this socially fulfilling perspective.

For Grandpa Morrsink, as for many workers, work helped define his class position and his cultural context.[12] While he may have sometimes viewed the behavior of bosses in terms of opposing class interests, he lived largely within what Chester Barnard called a psychological "zone of indifference."[13] That is, while workers appreciate a supportive and empowering approach from management, and will fight back if abuse becomes intolerable, they tend to tolerate a certain level of managerial disrespect as the logical consequence of the bureaucratic principles of large organizations. Only when working conditions become profoundly denigrating do workers develop, as a protective armor, a deep sense of class consciousness.

---

12 Alan Fox, *A Sociology of Work in Industry* (London: Collier MacMillan Ltd., 1971).

13 Chester Barnard, *The Functions of the Executive* (London: Oxford University Press, 1956).

In the white-collar, knowledge-based work environment, where people change jobs an average of once every four years, solidarity within the peer group has lost ground to a more individualistic ideology of monetary advancement and career advancement.[14] This *calculative orientation* gives feudal rewards to those who embrace a feudalistic ethos of loyalty, trust, fear, and obedience, while employers maintain only a short-term commitment to employees and retain the right to dismiss them at any time.

Organizational Climates

Many management theorists emphasize the need for a positive interface between organizations and individual employees. Thus, Noer advocates an organizational climate where employees are unencumbered by fear, false expectations of promotions, or the distractions of office politics.[15] He describes the ideal working environment as one that gives employees "the opportunity to harness their human spirit to work that they perceive as relevant and meaningful." In a similar vein, Bedeian and Armenakis warn of the potential "cesspool syndrome" that may occur in organizations that fixate on the cost of labor and lose sight of the energy and innovation that motivated workers can bring to the competitive process.[16]

---

14 Since Emile Durkheim first wrote about the dangers of anomie as a function of moral isolation and the loss of a "collective conscience," many social scientists have warned about urban malaise and loneliness. It is clear that recent technological developments, designed to create new linkages, have at the same time fostered new forms of isolation and atomization. Adrift in the global village, we forget how to interact with our next-door neighbor.

15 David M. Noer, *Breaking Free: A prescription for personal and organizational change* (San Francisco: Jossey-Bass, 1996). Fear is a major weapon in the arsenal of motivational techniques. It is used not only by almost all parents (even against their own better judgment), but it is also the most basic and enduring motivating method in organizations. Fear and insecurity, in tension with the interactional need for trust, are grossly neglected issues in organizational literature.

16 Arthur G. Bedian and Achilles A. Armenakis, "The Cesspool Syndrome: How dreck floats to top of declining organizations," *The Academy of Management Executive* 12 (1998): 58-67.

Pfeffer maintains that it is only through people that organizations exist and perform. He argues that long-term profitability is the result of focusing first and foremost on people.[17] High-performance management systems are sabotaged by the norms and influences in American corporate culture, which equate "good" management with being "mean and tough" and emphasize fear as the core motivator: "Putting people first means having articulated values and goals, organizational language and terminology, measurements, role models in senior leadership positions, and specific practices that make real the noble sentiments so often honored in the breach."[18]

Seligman addresses the problem of trust within the broad context of the civil society and the need for organizing life in the form of contractual associations. He defines trust in terms of social structure, relying heavily on the category of roles as the fundamental unit within an economy based on the division of labor. In this sense, trust can be understood as an interactional property expressed by people in relation to their social environment.[19]

Underlying all of these works is a common worldview: Employees are individuals with unique needs and motivations whose value transcends purely economic measurement. When the worker's dignity is established at the outset, it becomes possible to manage and evaluate employees in a positive, interactive way.

On the other hand, a reductive managerial approach that fails to acknowledge the wholeness and humanity of workers inevitably leads to indignity. Promotions or demotions based solely on a standardized, impersonal checklist represent bureaucracy at its worst. They provide no real sense of success for workers who get promoted and add insult to injury to those who lose out. Such mechanistic executive behavior (also seen in mandatory sentencing guidelines) promotes a brutal, unforgiving sort of "fairness."

Most scholars of organizational dynamics emphasize the link between the treatment of individual employees and the long-term

---

17 Jeffrey Pfeffer, *The Human Equation: Building profits by putting people first* (Cambridge: Harvard Business School Press, 1998).

18 Ibid.

19 Adam B. Seligman, *The Problem of Trust* (New Haven: Princeton University Press, 1997).

success of the organization. This connection is captured in such catchphrases as "people are our most important asset." Many studies indicate that while American institutions give lip service to such notions, managers too often persist in thinking in terms of power plays, short-term financial goals, and labor costs.

The forces of modernity and bureaucracy encourage uniformity, replaceability, and impersonality. Therefore, the indignities of the workplace—the persistent and common failure of the organization to view its employees as unique human beings—have become a ubiquitous feature of American organizational life. The modern worker is still at grave risk of becoming indistinguishable and disposable. We still internalize and socialize indignity as we learn to "lie low" and "go with the flow." Cartoonists (Scott Adams, creator of *Dilbert*, is perhaps the prime example) thrive on our culture's need to find relief from stifling bureaucracy by joking about indignity.

Why should we expect something as intangible as dignity to be integrated into the workings of the contemporary organization? Businesses and other organizations are not, after all, Mr. Rogers' neighborhood. They do not view the building of workers' self-esteem as their raison d'être.

The answer is that dignity is not a frill. When employees feel good about their work, the organization benefits. In a dignifying organization, where employees are genuinely perceived as assets rather than costs, motivation is high and the work environment is stimulating. Management and employees meet challenges together. When competition is structured and controlled, people learn to cooperate, seek coalitions, and accept outcomes gracefully.

In sports, healthy competitiveness is referred to as sportsmanship; in politics, statesmanship; and in business, respect for the competition. Parliamentary governments and democracy itself are made possible by the concept of loyal opposition. Adversaries within such a system may be bitterly at odds with each others' politics, but maintain a bedrock respect for the rules of the game and the democratic legitimacy of the other party.

Research shows, however, that few corporate cultures embody this healthy, restrained competitiveness. Too often, rivalry within and between organizations is conceptualized as total war, in which, as Oscar Wilde noted, "It's not enough to win; the others have to fail."

Indignity is the natural result of the warlike rivalry between and within modern bureaucratic organizations, in the context of a society increasingly devoid of any sense of community. The very concept of *organizational dignity* is often perceived as an oxymoron. "If you're looking for dignity in the workplace," one colleague told us, "you're out of luck. That's the last place you'll find it." In our hundreds of interviews over the past several years with factory and office workers, physicians, consultants, bankers, policemen, attorneys, government employees, professors, and others, almost all subjects could cite workplace incidents that they considered indignities, while very few could recall even a single dignifying experience.

Not only blue-collar workers, but unskilled laborers, white-collar workers, and professionals all suffer indignities. Indignities can be institutionalized in forms such as racism and sexism. Denigration today knows no class or gender boundaries. Most employees seem to feel that the indignities of organizational life, large and small, must be accepted and tolerated. Workers can do little more than try to avoid high blood pressure and work-related stress syndrome, while hoping they will eventually even the score.

Society encourages us to believe that indignity is the norm, a perquisite of power. Superiors are free to motivate with fear and humiliation, and employees are bound to accept these methods.[20] Middle managers perhaps suffer the most, as they lack the power of senior executives and are generally unprotected by unions or protective labor laws. It is no wonder that many stories about indignity involve middle managers, who are passing on to those who report to them the indignities to which they themselves are subjected.

Dignity is not a legal concept, but rather part of the value system from which laws are derived. Nor is dignity precisely a human right. To say that workers, including managers, have a right to be treated

---

[20] Within a certain context, such as a military boot camp, motivation through humiliation may be effective, but it is always expressly denigrating, abusing the individual's need for dignity. David A. DeCenzo and Stephen P. Robbins, *Human Resource Management* (New York: Wiley, 1996). See also Chapter Four.

with dignity is to misunderstand the concept. It would be analogous to claiming that spouses have the right to be loved. Such a right does not exist, as love cannot be demanded or even directly observed. But without love, however defined, marriages will eventually fail or become empty shells.

It is the same with organizations and dignity. Workers engage in long-term relationships with organizations. Within those relationships, employees don't have a "right" to dignity—but without manifestations of dignity, employees will lose their motivation and commitment. In such an environment, employees stay on the payroll by default, until they can find a better situation elsewhere.

Subtleties of Dignity

The lengthy and popular lyrics of Bob Dylan's 1994 song "Dignity," speak of a never-ending search for dignity. Dylan cites several examples of how subtle and elusive it is, but the fact that dignity is subtle does not render it any less real.[21] For example, love, respect, and self-esteem may not be easily explained, but they remain incredibly powerful forces. We live in an era of self-help movements and psychological theories that stress independence and self-reliance.[22] Self-esteem movements aim to bolster our sense of inner worth to the point of invulnerability. The American Association of University Women argues that girls must be assertive and competitive to survive in the modern business world. Our culture broadcasts the message that we all matter, each and every one of us, in atomized isolation.

Emphasis on individualism and self-sufficiency has fueled the idea that the key to happiness is to steel oneself from the influence of others. We have learned to develop mental shields. Our heroes, glorified in literature and film, are invulnerable loners, who stand apart from society. The idealization of self-sufficiency dates back at

---

21 Bob Dylan, "Dignity," *Bob Dylan's Greatest Hits Vol. 3*, Sony.

22 Increasingly, healthcare professionals realize that this individualistic approach is egocentric and can be ineffective in many types of interventions.

least to Socrates, whose goal was to make sure nothing could touch him.[23]

In reality, we are all affected by how others treat us. We exist in society, and we are bound together by powerful ties of shared needs, values, and aspirations. How we regard others and how they regard us is a vital component of what constitutes human identity and interaction. If we can see others always as fellow human beings, fundamentally equal to ourselves, then we can partake in dignifying relationships. The notion that dignity is not an innate personal characteristic, but rather one that is conferred upon us through relationships, is reflected in our speech patterns. For example, in the spring of 1996, news reports described the death of a severely obese woman. While neighbors, including children, watched, police officers dragged the body by the heels from the house, laughing and making crude remarks. One neighbor commented aptly, "They did not give her any dignity at all."

Dignity and indignity are bestowed upon us by others, even after death. If dignity overrides other considerations in death, should it not have even more importance in the affairs of everyday life? Certainly, the price of ignoring dignity can be very high, as we see in the growing violence associated with disgruntled workers.

The relatively recent focus on employee empowerment—that is, an organizational culture in which workers can take greater initiative—has made some managers aware of the need to reduce denigration in the workplace. However, dignity is *not* empowerment. Nor is it "good supervision," "job enrichment," "change for growth," "improvement," or "advancement." These are all techniques. Dignity is a fundamental value, and dignifying is a fundamental social activity. While dignity can be developed and encouraged, it cannot be managed the way an employee training program or human resources plan can be. Dignity or denigration comes into play every time people within an organization interact with one another.

Dignifying is by no means confined to the workplace. Dignifying and its opposite occur in *all* social environments, including families, religious groups, clubs, and schools. Children are socialized to the

---

23 Martha C. Nussbaum, *The Fragility of Goodness: Luck and Ethics in Greek Tragedy and Philosophy* (London: Cambridge University Press, 1986).

accepted notion of dignity through the family, learning rules like "honor your elders so that you may be honored in time."

Rules like this, misapplied, can lead to behavior that is not dignifying. A man from Nigeria, for example, related the story of how in his British-modeled junior high school, he suffered greatly from the many insults that the seniors were allowed to bestow upon him, while he had to "honor" their rank and status. The next year, he was delighted to insult the juniors in the same way. He had fallen into the socializing trap that the British school system maintains in order to prepare the pupils for a rigidly organized, class-conscious society.

This example illustrates the continued application of feudal models of dignity, which fits the hierarchical structure of the corporate bureaucracy and the patriarchal model of the traditional family. Many institutions fail to adopt the ethos of democratic dignifying, whereby each individual is considered uniquely valuable, and where people exist, not as a means to achieve someone else's end, but as ends in themselves.

The feudal indignities and denigrations found in organizations are the by-product of managerial strategies influenced by what might be called "Fordism," the highly mechanized, efficiency-driven, command-and-control model championed by Henry Ford. These strategies create and perpetuate three varieties of indignity. The first variety, which we call the "Sisyphusean Paradigm," is a by-product of the alienating conditions of production within large bureaucratic organizations. The second type of indignity exists at the level of corporate climate, culture, and communication. An unhealthy climate or culture can permit indignities or encourage passivity on the part of victims of denigration. The third and most easily identified variety of indignity stems from inequalities in power within the organization. At this level, rude or even illegal behavior is tolerated due to workers' relative lack of power and influence.

The Sisyphusean Paradigm

Sisyphus, a character in Greek mythology, angered the gods and was compelled to spend eternity rolling a boulder uphill. He could never complete his task because the boulder would roll back to the base of the mountain as Sisyphus neared the summit. Sisyphus' fate was perpetual futility.

The myth, conceived thousands of years ago, still resonates. The real punishment of Sisyphus is not continuous hard work—it is hard work without meaning. No conscious being with freedom of choice would be happy with such a fate. It is the essence of absurdity. Yet the industrial economy condemns many workers in pursuit of a paycheck to perform tasks that are essentially meaningless.

When Adam Smith observed that manufacturers could increase productivity by dividing processes into small tasks and repeated movements, he unwittingly unlinked, or alienated, workers from their product, condemning them to a Sisyphusean fate. Accepting this alienation as a normal and unavoidable consequence of greater efficiency was the first step in the culture of industrialization.[24]

Large-scale mass production transformed society, vastly expanding the alienation of labor. Max Weber, a pioneering sociologist, analyzed the dynamics of decision-making in the modern organization and saw that alienation was inherent in bureaucracy.[25] Weber did not like what he foresaw, and warned of malaise and an eventual erosion of civic society.[26]

Most studies of workplace alienation and impersonal behavior have focused on blue-collar workers. A vast amount of research shows that, at the organizational level, these dynamics are associated with enormous losses in terms of money, time, social well-being, and even human lives. Much of the unprecedented suffering experienced in the twentieth century can be linked to the fallout of alienation and bureaucratization unleashed by a deformed vision of efficiency.

The routinization of work and the conditioning of blue-collar employees to mechanized work represent a denial of dignity at a deep level. Issues of dignity may arise during open labor conflict

---

24 Adam Smith, *Wealth of Nations* (New York: The Modern Library, 1937).

25 Hans H. Gerth and C. Wright Mills, *From Max Weber: Essays in Sociology* (London: Routledge and Kegan Paul Ltd., 1948).

26 Richard M. Merelman, "On Legitimalaise in the United States: A Weberian Analysis," *The Sociological Quarterly* 39 (1998): 351-368.

or union negotiations, but once the strike is over and the contract is signed, dignity often declines as a management priority.

William Whyte, author of *The Organization Man*, was among the first to address these issues for the growing mass of white-collar workers.[27] He noted that people within organizations tend to view themselves as "objects more acted upon than acting—and their future, therefore, determined as much by the system as by themselves." Since this landmark book was published in the 1950s, there has been some change for the better for some workers, but much has stayed the same. The value systems that drive alienation and impersonal behavior are still with us; they are ingrained in our culture and even our psyche.

It is tempting to regard these destructive value systems as the "natural consequence" of organizational life. However, we should not let organizations and managers off the hook so easily. Organizations are man-made arrangements, and their social dynamics can be rethought and retooled. Social science has provided significant insights into improving organizational life, and one can point to many successful applications of these ideas. We know that in humane organizations, the individual employee is viewed as an essential part of the whole, and work projects are organized in such a way as to encourage a sense of ownership and teamwork. It is the job of the social sciences to keep management's feet to the fire in terms of social responsibility and human dignity.

Paradoxes and contradictions abound, and should be noted and condemned. For instance, some companies spend thousands of dollars training employees in the fine art of face-saving during conflicts, then turn around and fire older workers, because they cost too much. That is indignity. Seldom does management perform a strategic analysis that takes into account factors that might mitigate in favor of greater dignification, such as social capital, experience, workforce morale, and company image. Instead, they content themselves with a simplistic wage comparison of fifty-year-old and thirty-year-old employees. There is hard evidence that the logic behind this decision

---

27 William H. Whyte, *The Organization of Man* (Garden City, NY: Simon and Schuster, Inc., 1956).

is wrong and shortsighted, yet companies continue to denigrate the older worker.

Whether or not such decisions are technically legal, they are morally and economically misguided. The vision of employees as interchangeable parts, to be fitted willy-nilly into a production or service process without consideration for the individual, is indignity in its purest form. However effective in terms of short-term moneymaking, it is a poor excuse for enterprise management.

The routinization of work is coupled with the age-old method of increasing productivity by resorting to motivational shortcuts such as fear and harassment. *The Electronic Sweatshop* describes how modern technology, combined with old-fashioned exploitive management techniques, leads to inhuman work rhythms. In such an environment, even highly motivated workers quickly become disillusioned, overstretched, and burned out.[28]

The Overworked American is another penetrating analysis of work and leisure time.[29] The book counters the common assumption that leisure time has increased while working hours have decreased, an idea based on a comparison with eighteenth- and nineteenth-century standards, when people labored under what Schor calls "probably the longest and most arduous work schedules in the history of humankind." Today, Schor reports, Americans are once again sleeping less, working longer hours, and finding less time for recreation and family togetherness—an imbalance damaging to the quality of both life and work. The proliferation of laptop computers, beepers, and cell phones means that many employees are essentially on-call twenty-four hours a day. The fast-track career mentality, with its compulsory job-hopping, self-marketing, and diploma collecting, adds to the pressure white-collar workers feel.

We have created organizational structures and reward mechanisms that leave people feeling depressed, insecure, and exhausted. The indignities and anxieties associated with traditional organizational

---

28 Barbara Garson, *The Electronic Sweatshop: How computers are transforming the office of the future into the factory of the past* (New York: Penguin USA, 1989).

29 Juliet B. Schor, *The Overworked American: The unexpected decline of leisure* (New York: Basic Books, 1992).

life are a serious economic, civic, and public health issue. Undoing the damage wrought by bureaucracy and blind rationality will require a radical rethinking of the role of the individual and the place of dignity within the organization.

> At a TGI Friday's restaurant in Harrisburg, Pennsylvania, forty full- and part-time workers come half an hour before their shift starts to attend motivational meetings with the restaurant manager. When there is a birthday, the manager provides a small party in the latter part of the shift. The manager has visited almost all of the workers at home at least once. The workers have organized daycare and babysitting schedules, as well as carpools and snow emergency transportation. Sickness and family illness issues are ironed out by the work group. Management participates in every aspect of restaurant operations to keep the workload evenly distributed, which has a major impact on the earning curves of everyone. Several years after graduation, student-servers with career-track jobs still come to work one or more nights each week.[30]
>
> The restaurant's managers have laid down some simple operating rules for staff:
>
> - Tell me when something is wrong, not someone else.
> - Respect and support your fellow team members.
> - Don't rely on me to figure out that you need something from me, tell me yourself.
> - Take credit and responsibility for your work.[31]

This management team works with an attitude that is dignifying. By promoting the unique contributions of each staff member, managers create a work atmosphere that is healthy and productive.

Sadly, this type of management is the exception, not the rule. Few organizations promote the positive and open dynamic required by a successful work team, and few managers possess the necessary

---

30 Personal observation.

31 These rules are borrowed and edited from a speech given by Dr. Cynthia Barnes Boyd in 1996.

degree of commitment. Managers may have heard such success stories at conferences and workshops, but they often do not know how to apply these lessons, or assume that such methods could not succeed in their organization. It is difficult to undo, even with example, the ingrained habits of a lifetime.

There are few organizations that have the vision to channel internal competition away from destructive turf wars and toward healthy, constructive goals. Competition is almost always thought of as a win-lose game, often with more losers than winners. Win-win management styles rely on dignifying attitudes that encourage respectful and energizing behaviors that flow from it. Such styles—like that of the Harrisburg TGI Friday's—require high levels of trust in others and in oneself.

All organizations have a climate, a culture. In all organizations, however complex, there is a dominant tone. Over time, organizations develop distinct personalities and are labeled accordingly (e.g., conservative or progressive, relaxed or rigid, communicative or secretive). Once labeled, an organization has to learn to live with its reputation, as customers, investors, workers, and other stakeholders expect consistent behavior.

The culture of an organization or business colors the behavior and perceptions of managers and employees, and cultural difference often leads to unintentional slights. For example, the fear of sexual harassment in the banking industry, with its large female workforce and thick glass ceilings, fosters an interaction tone that resulted in an unusual complaint from an Italian banker temporarily assigned to an American branch. After six weeks in New York, she became confused and insecure about her femininity because none of her male colleagues complimented her, made a pass at her, or in any other way acknowledged her gender. The preferred American method of dealing with workplace diversity is to ignore the obvious and pretend to be colorblind and sexless. In other cultures, where zero tolerance rules are unfamiliar, these issues are dealt with more openly through dialogue or group evaluations.

The lesson here is that there will always be moments at work which are dignifying and not dignifying. However, these experiences are often in the eye of the beholder and resistant to generalization.

For example, one man stated that he began a job reporting to a jovial supervisor who displayed a "manly use" of language, cursing colorfully and often. Within weeks, his wife noticed that his own language had deteriorated badly. People tend to adapt to their environment, and so the employee started to communicate at home as he did at work. Abusive language in the workplace did not constitute indignity, since it was shared by all, but it was perceived as denigrating by family members. Indignity is often relative to milieu, and workers are rarely able to influence the standards of civility that govern the shop floor or office.

Who is responsible for setting the tone of an organization? Deetz argues that organizations are "talked into being."[32] That is, all who participate in organizational discourse set the tone, not only those in authority. How then is it possible to change an organization's tone, when it emanates from more than one source? We may find an answer in Peter French's analysis of where moral responsibility resides within an organization. Rebutting the common argument that only individuals can have responsibility, and not organizations, masses, or other groups, French traces responsibility back to what he calls the "corporate decision" structure. In many cases, no single person has ultimate responsibility: strategy and policy are determined by the composite actions of many people.[33]

Voices at different levels of authority, acting in concert, shape an organization's tone, style, and climate. Efforts to change a tone or culture will be stronger and longer-lasting when they originate with those in the organization who have large spans of control. However, even at the bottom of the organizational totem pole, there is fertile ground for culture change, although the immediate impact may be limited. Any such initiative, however, needs a nurturing response throughout the organization. Without active managerial support for change, organizations will soon revert to the lowest common denominators: fear, greed, and jealousy.

---

32 S. Deetz, "Critical Interpretive Research in Organizational Communication," *Western Journal of Speech Communication* 46 (1982): 131-49.

33 Peter A. French, *Responsibility Matters* (Kansas: University Press of Kansas, 1994).

Power and Indignity

The close affinity between power, abuse, and indignity has its roots in the feudal concept of dignity, where some have dignity and others do not, reflecting the social stratification of society. This feudal concept lingers on in modern organizations, most of which are inherently undemocratic and use various symbolisms to underscore inequality. Two-way dignifying is not at home in such an environment.

Our experience with indignity begins in earliest childhood. Youngsters begin the process of socialization from a position of powerlessness and dependence. We can all recall incidents from our early days when we were denied a voice—when our opinion not only did not count, but was not even heard. The patriarchal model of the family is mirrored in our thinking about organizations and is even translated into law. In structure, language, and process, our legal system revolves around the power of possession, including the possession of thoughts and ideas. We reify intangibles, transforming *being* into *having*. For power in our society resides in having, and we all learn early that disrespecting power, even for the sake of being whole, has dire consequences.

Abuse of power and denigration are rarely arbitrary; they are linked to environments or cultures that tolerate or even promote such behavior. Racism, sexism, and disregard for the dignity of the disabled were long viewed not as problems, but as the natural order of things. Not so long ago, it was normal for bosses to hit workers as a motivating tactic. Drill sergeants in the army were often of the opinion that you had to "break 'em before you fix 'em."

Status-linked arrogance and insult are still strongly in evidence, showing how far we have to go before we can attain a truly democratic notion of dignity. Many clients enter a service relationship with an over-inflated sense of importance, throwing their weight around in obnoxious fashion. Stories of abusive celebrity behavior are legion, exemplified by actress Zsa Zsa Gabor's well-publicized slapping of a police officer after receiving a ticket for a traffic violation. (She was arrested and later sentenced and fined.) Celebrities are themselves plagued by tabloid hacks and paparazzi, who often behave like flies on a carcass, justifying their disregard of basic human dignity by claiming that they supply a market. When we accept the invisible hand of the market as a totalitarian force, untrammeled by morality, civil society is in danger.

Our concept of power, defined as the ability to influence or direct the behavior of others, even against their will, reflects the core reality of institutionalized inequality.[34] Can the notion of democratic dignifying be reconciled with this ever-present dynamic of power inequality? It is worth considering several points related to this topic.

Power within organizations is not absolute and should not be treated as absolute. More often than not, inequality is an accepted and, to some extent, negotiated arrangement between parties. If power imbalances become unbearable, employees sometimes have viable means of contesting the imbalance, including protests, lawsuits, staging a strike or slowdown, or simply quitting. Successful organizations engage in periodic "healthy questioning" of top leadership to spur performance and prevent stagnation.

Public opinion is another limiting factor on power. While Americans tend to admire successful businesspeople, the public and its elected representatives can trim down to size tycoons who overstep the boundaries of acceptable conduct. For example, a Senate hearing in 1998 subjected Microsoft CEO Bill Gates, the richest man in the world, to harsh criticism. One of the damning comments made about Gates was that he had developed an arrogant attitude.

Power in organizations is invested in certain roles; these roles are increasingly based on specialized knowledge. The increasing importance of knowledge as the basis of power (rather than force or wealth) changes human interactions in fundamental ways.[35] Knowledge is inseparable from the worker, providing employees with greater leverage than that of the traditional laborer. Furthermore, knowledge must be used and shared to be effective. Finally, knowledge is more fluid than traditional job skills; workers must accumulate knowledge continually to stay current, move ahead professionally, and maintain their importance to the organization.

---

34 Gerth and Mills, 1948.

35 Alvin Toffler, *Powershift: Knowledge, Wealth and Violence at the Edge of the 21st Century* (New York: Bantam Books, 1990).

Employee empowerment programs, which encourage workers to claim discretionary authority and responsibility for their decisions, are one result of this professionalization paradigm. Business schools now offer classes in the field of managing "prima donna" employees. The knowledge revolution is ushering in a new era of redesigned roles in which the power dynamic of inequality, while by no means disappearing, will be less of a factor in setting the terms of organizational behavior.

The labor laws of recent decades have focused on harassment, discrimination, and other blameful actions by those in positions of power. In coming years, the acquisition of productive knowledge by workers will bring about a fundamental redistribution of corporate power. The legal phase of fighting denigration of women and minorities will give way as managers recognize the indispensability and power of the knowledge worker. In the knowledge-driven workplace, respect for dignity will take on new meaning and broader scope for managers and workers alike.

###

Chapter Three

Managerial Mindsets and Their Impact on Dignity

There are a few governing principles, and before considering their application in detail we should think first about the file. He is a Man; he expects to be treated as an adult, not as a schoolboy. He has rights; they must be made known to him and thereafter respected. He has ambition; it must be stirred. He has a belief in fair play; it must be honored. He has the need for comradeship; it must be supplied. He has imagination; it must be stimulated. He has a sense of personal dignity; it must not be broken down. He has pride; it can be satisfied and made the bedrock of his character once he gains assurance that he is playing a useful and respected part in a superior and successful organization. To give men working as a group the feeling of great accomplishment together is the acme of inspired leadership.

In the degree that the disciplinary method and the training procedure of the military service, and the common sense of his superiors, combine to nourish these satisfactions in the individual, esprit de corps comes into being . . . He becomes loyal because loyalty has been given to him. He learns to serve an ideal because an ideal has served him . . .

— From *The Armed Forces Officer*[36]

As with army officers, so with managers. Managing an organization is more than a matter of improving productivity and profits—the organization is a crucible for the development and enhancement of human potential and dignity. This concept of management's role, however, is often denied, dismissed, or derided, the victim of certain managerial mindsets that hinder the development

---

[36] Department of Defense, United States Government Printing Office. *The Armed Forces Officer.* 1950.

of dignifying workplace relationships. This chapter describes these pervasive and destructive mindsets.

The Four Major Mindsets

Just as styles of management and working are set in a social context, so theories about work and organization reflect broader social paradigms. We attribute and evaluate facts and fiction in a given context.[37] For instance, the assumption that nature is something to be controlled, rather than adapted to, belongs to what could be called the realm of socially bounded rationality, reflecting current cultural premises. As societies have confronted the impact of industrial production and modern transportation on the environment, this assumption about nature has given ground somewhat to varying forms of environmentalism that recognize the need for human adaptation to the natural world.

Context changes with time and circumstances. When we can accept change as a constant, and cultural context as relative, then we are in a position to examine our assumptions and alter them to achieve new purposes and reflect new values. Change is driven by a variety of factors, including science, technology, and demographics. In our own time, we have come to understand change as the energy that drives our ability to tackle the problems of daily living. Indeed, change has become an ideology, a unifying explanatory concept.

Individuals generally think of their changing assessments of context as a sign of intellectual and moral development, not as the correction of a mistake. Each of us has a dominant mindset through which we judge our own actions and opinions and those of others. While people can develop different mindsets for different contexts, they must have some overall consistency of values. Culture is a driving force behind our mindsets. We can understand and respond to the mindsets of others in our society because we have been exposed to many of the same socializing forces.

But society is neither monolithic nor conflict-free. Examining the cultural and taste differences between classes, Pierre Bourdieu

---

[37] Geoffrey Vickers, *The Art of Judgment: A study of policy making* (London: Chapman and Hall Ltd., 1995).

developed the concept of *habitus* to describe how social forces affect our personalities, tastes, and habits.[38] According to Bourdieu, our habitus both anchors us in our social world and limits our freedom and choice in many areas. Bourdieu's concept explains why members of different classes tend to have different opinions on politics, religion, and culture, as well as variant food preferences and buying habits. Our mindset and habitus are constantly in the background, influencing our particular positions and attitudes. Incorporating opposing views into our mindsets may feel like an act of liberation from our past and our anchoring concepts. However, some may view this fluidity not as liberation but as heresy or error, and seek to enforce conformity by coercing dissidents to abide by their own mindsets. (The ongoing debate about "political correctness," for instance, reflects conflict over our changing normative mindset regarding cultural diversity.)

A review of the scholarly literature on the subject suggests four ideal-type models of managerial mindsets that have long dominated the work environment in western society, diminishing human dignity within organizations.[39] The four major mindsets, which profoundly influence how managers perceive workers, are:

- the bureaucratic mindset (Boxes on an Org Chart)
- the production line mindset (Cogs in a Wheel)
- the military mindset (Privates in a Boot Camp)
- the social science mindset (Lab Rats of the Social Scientist)

These mindsets, which developed during the Industrial Revolution, can be linked philosophically to the tenets of nineteenth-century British empiricism—many of which have been

38 Pierre Bourdieu, *Distinction: A social critique of the judgment of taste*, translated by Richard Nice (Cambridge: Harvard University Press, 1984).

39 The term "ideal-type" refers to the notion, in social sciences, of constructing a non-real model in order to understand phenomena in the real world. Max Weber has used this method to describe bureaucracy and capitalism, and Jurgen Habermas has used it to describe the ideal speech communication. The ideal-type of a free market, for example, does not exist in reality but drives almost all of our economic policies, such as anti-trust legislation.

rendered obsolete by twentieth-century scientific and technological developments. However, cultural attitudes tend to persist longer than the conditions that produce them. With the onset of the knowledge revolution, these mindsets need to be re-examined.

Most large organizations are now feeling the effects of globalization and knowledge-based specialization, and managerial mindsets are beginning to adapt to these new forces. The rate of change seems to be accelerating, leading writers such as Peter Drucker to talk about a state of perpetual fluidity. We can, in a sense, harness these changes by developing new mindsets that foster human dignity. Managers must learn to *see* in new ways. It is the task of management and labor, individually and collectively, to put dignity on the agenda and to develop mindsets that reconcile human and organizational needs.

The Bureaucratic Mindset (Boxes on an Org Chart)

The bureaucratic mindset refers to the structured way of thinking that Americans have learned both to perfect and to hate. The bureaucratic mentality underlies many common features of organizational life, such as merit pay increases, universal pension plans, and internal career ladders. The bureaucratic manager sees the worker as a "human resource" and encourages employees to see themselves as accumulations of "human capital."

This mentality, which translates everything into data and puts these data in boxes on an organizational chart, is responsible for taking the existing notion of a corporate purpose and distilling it into over-detailed job descriptions and nebulous mission statements. It boils down complex ideas of morality and values into standardized codes of ethics and conformist corporate etiquette. It turns the intensely personal interaction during performance evaluations into a numbing annual routine aimed primarily at reducing exposure to lawsuits, and uses "company policy" as a universal elixir against the risk of taking personal responsibility.

This is the mindset that distributes posters, organizational newsletters, wallet cards, and motivational calendars to employees, but never reaches out to employees in a personal way. It is responsible for snatching at every hot new idea, transforming it into a quick-fix management slogan, implementing it poorly, then moving on to the next management fad. It keeps hoisting new flags on the same boats, but never dares think about open seas and fast clippers.

To the bureaucratic mindset, the concept of democratic dignity is anathema. Dignity is about open, inclusive relationships between bosses, workers, and clients. Bureaucracy is about exclusion, turf wars, power trips, blame games, and buck-passing. Bureaucracy provides the tools to hide behind a title or rule, protecting against the exposure of open work relations, where individuals must earn respect.

Early in the century, Max Weber described several characteristics of a bureaucracy that still hold true today. First, official responsibilities within the organization are fixed, and require some degree of specialization to be carried out effectively. Second, duties are arranged hierarchically: authority flows downward while accountability flows upward. Third, the day-to-day workings of the organization are governed by formal policies that are applied to individual cases to produce the desired uniformity. Fourth, bureaucrats ideally carry out their responsibilities impersonally. Personal considerations are sacrificed in the name of an impartial and efficient system. Later research clearly shows that bureaucrats are not as static or impersonal as the model suggests.

Bureaucracies have their advantages, to be sure. They were established to improve rationality and make decision-making less dependent on the whims of kings and other arbitrary rulers. Bureaucracies impart a degree of stability to organizations, allowing long-term planning and predictable implementation. It is bureaucracy that enables mail to be delivered around the globe in a set time for a fixed fee, no matter the mood of the letter carrier. When bureaucracy works, it delivers a consistent product or service. As an executive of a fast food company once put it, "We don't want everyone reinventing the way to make a cheeseburger." Indeed, many Americans abroad never think twice about the fact that they can buy identical Big Macs in Brazil, Japan, Germany, and Surinam.

On the other hand, bureaucratic mindsets tend to detach workers from the purpose and meaning of their work. As R. K. Merton writes, "Adherence to the rules, originally conceived as a means, becomes transformed into an end in itself; there occurs the familiar process of the displacement of goals whereby an instrumental value becomes a terminal value."[40] Similarly, Anthony Downs describes how the pool of bureaucrats within an organization changes over time, as "zealots" give way to "conformists" and "conservers."[41]

In bureaucracies, leaving one's mark on the organization or improving production or service capabilities becomes less important than simply following instructions. Says one office manager of a small company, "When I was hired, I was told that they really needed me to come and 'shake things up around here.' But now, after a year, I've only managed to change one buying process and one vendor contract. Everything else I've suggested has been shot down. I'm totally stifled."

The bureaucratic mindset is one of the major reasons why so many people feel alienated from their work. The general sense of ennui and gloom manifests itself in publications with names like *The Search for Meaning in the Workplace* or *The Careless Society*. People's growth is stifled because they feel boxed in, small, and unable to make a difference. Many middle managers believe they are more likely to earn a promotion if they avoid making waves,

---

40 Robert K. Merton, "Notes on Problem Finding in Sociology," in *Sociology Today*, eds. Merton, et al. (New York: Basic Books Inc., 1959), pp. xv-xvi.

41 Anthony Downs, *Inside Bureaucracy* (Chicago: Waveland Press, 1966).

and rationalize that they will "shake things up" once they have been promoted and have more power. In the end, however, each box, no matter how high on the org chart, corresponds to a set of rules, regulations, and sanctions that discourage managers at all levels from making waves.

Bureaucracies degrade integrity and self-worth. New hires are dangerous to the status quo if they seek to make their own unique contribution, and are subject to animosity from their peers if they try too hard. They get the cold shoulder if they cannot or will not adhere to the conditions and expectations of their box.

Bureaucrats learn to live in fear. A director of a local chapter of a national professional association notes the "tension, distrust, and fear" that characterize his work environment. Particularly interesting was his description of the monthly management meeting, presided over by the CEO:

> The meetings consisted primarily of monologues by the CEO. On the whole, managers (not just the middle managers, but also the three or four executive staff who made up the CEO's inner circle) were afraid to say what was on their minds at these meetings. They were afraid, for example, to express their sense of confusion about the service delivery principles being discussed. The priorities seemed to change from month to month, depending on the most recent communication from the national organization. Priorities also changed depending on management's perception of how the organization could link its name with whatever topic was currently "hot" in the field.
>
> Managers who directed functional departments were in conflict with those responsible for the territory-based districts. Expressing concern or asking for help on issues was simply an invitation for ridicule from the CEO. Everyone had experienced this at one time or another, and no one felt like having it happen to him again.

> Managers were fearful of appearing to be incompetent or even mistaken. The result was that few of us spoke up at management meetings. Mostly, we just listened respectfully, unless we spoke up merely to endorse the CEO's position on this or that. Then we went back to our desks and quietly complained to our colleagues. Conflicts did not get resolved in an enduring way, and priorities remained unclear. Much energy was consumed in efforts to resolve role conflicts, and service delivery responded to crises with little or no sense of strategic direction.[42]

The attitude of this particular CEO clearly contributed to the atmosphere of fear and apathy among the managers. It is also important to see how the bureaucratic context prevented managers from joining forces against the CEO. The bureaucratic mindset not only stifles initiative, it also overvalues respect for authority and hierarchical decision-making. Americans like to scorn the bureaucratic mindset—witness the constant bashing of bureaucracy by politicians and the media. Few critics note, however, the extent to which bureaucracies mold almost everyone's character, including their own.

The bureaucratic mindset can have a subtle negative impact even in seemingly healthy and positive environments, such as organizations that enjoy a high degree of consensus and cohesiveness. Irving Janis warns against the dangers of *groupthink*, defined as "a mode of thinking that people engage in when they are deeply involved in a cohesive in-group, when the members' striving for unanimity overrides their motivation to realistically appraise alternative courses of action." Janis also associates

Eight Symptoms of Groupthink:

- Excessive self-censorship
- Illusions of unanimity
- Direct pressure put on dissenters
- Self-appointed mind guards
- Illusions of group invulnerability
- Belief in the inherent morality of the group
- Collective rationalizations
- Stereotypes of out-groups

(Janis, *Groupthink*, 1992)

42 Personal interview.

groupthink with "a deterioration of mental efficiency, reality testing, and moral judgment that results from in-group pressures."[43] In such an environment, workers and managers, according to Janis, encounter cognitive and structural constraints that interfere with their problem-solving skills. Experience in the harsh realities of organizational life turns almost every worker and executive toward the path of concurrence-seeking. This involves erasing one's uniqueness as an individual out of a desire to agree always with the majority—even if that means embracing counterproductive, unethical, or absurd practices. Bureaucrats do not rock the boat, and they make sure that their subordinates do not either. Not being seen and not seeing others as whole human beings—invisibility and blindness—become virtues, negating people's deep-seated need for recognition and comradeship.

Many efforts have been made to counter the destructive effects of the bureaucratic mindset, but they remain pervasive. Practices such as employee empowerment, reengineering, and horizontal management were intended to reduce bureaucracy, but instead reinforced it, according to Charles Heckscher.[44] Says Heckscher, "Restructuring not only fails to create new forms of participation, it destroys old forms of participation that kept good bureaucracies working reasonably well in the past." In other words, empowerment (as implemented) has eliminated the positive aspects of bureaucracy, such as stability and continuity, without creating new and better organizational structures and relationships. According to Heckscher, "The problem is [employees] no longer have the network of trusting relationships so crucial in the past. They cope by withdrawing into a narrow world, putting their heads down, getting by, waiting it out."

When a technique or label is adopted, but the underlying ideas are not, the result is frustration, confusion, and eventual failure. Empowerment attempted to create self-directed work teams that had a very limited mandate and that operated within the space allotted

---

43 Irving Janis, *Groupthink: Psychological studies of policy decisions and fiascoes* (Boston: Houghton Mifflin, 1982), 9.

44 Charles Heckscher and Anne Donnellon, eds., *Post-bureaucratic organization: New perspectives on organizational change* (Thousand Oaks: Sage Publications, 1994).

on the org chart. On the one hand, we see peers seeking to arrive at consensus; on the other hand, a still-dominant hierarchy. Empowerment became a technique used by the bureaucracy, rather than a challenge to the bureaucratic mindset. Because most empowerment programs do not build upon the uniqueness of each worker, they cannot rectify the harm done by bureaucratic mentality.

There is no trendy, easy solution to the problem of the bureaucratic mindset. Only by respecting the dignity and worth of the individual employee can the negative effects of bureaucratic functioning be overcome. Teams cannot be "empowered" while people continue to be denigrated.

The Production Line Mindset (Cogs in a Wheel)

This mindset views employees as mere replaceable parts of a more important whole. The organization is perceived as a giant wheel that turns of itself, somehow apart from and beyond the efforts of individuals. This perspective also goes back to the Industrial Revolution and its ground-breaking idea of dividing complex processes into simple, repetitive motions. "The greatest improvement in the productive powers of labour," wrote Adam Smith in *Wealth of Nations*, "and the greater part of the skill, dexterity, and judgment with which it is directed or applied, seem to have been the effect of the division of labour."[45] Smith provides the famous example of the pin-making worker:

> A workman not educated to this business (which the division of labour has rendered a distinct trade), not acquainted with the use of machinery employed in it (to the invention of which the same division of labour has probably given occasion), could scarce, perhaps, with his utmost industry, make one pin in a day, and certainly could not make twenty. But in the way in which this business is now carried on, not only the

---

[45] Smith, 1937. What Adam Smith called *division of labor* is referred to here as *separation of tasks*. This prevents confusion with Emile Durkheim's use of the phrase *division of labor*, which he defines as the process by which society assigns tasks and roles to different groups and individuals.

whole work is a peculiar trade, but it is divided into a number of branches, of which the greater part are likewise peculiar trades. One man draws out the wire, another straightens it, a third cuts it, a fourth points it, a fifth grinds it at the top for receiving the head: to make the head requires two or three distinct operations; to put it on is a peculiar business, to whiten the pins is another; it is even a trade by itself to put them into the paper; and the important business of making a pin is, in this manner, divided into about eighteen distinct operations, which in some manufactories are all performed by distinct hands, though in others the same man will sometimes perform two or three of them.

> The scheduling and operations manager of a trucking company with more than two hundred drivers complains bitterly about production line mindset of his CEO. He had to deal with the Teamster's local. This was not a problem, as he knew all the truckers and their particular needs and wishes, and he could run the whole system at a profit. The CEO, however, saw only trucks, routes, down times, and riding times and had no clue about the human aspect of trucking. His willful ignorance of the human dynamic led to a constant pressure for streamlined, data-driven, more efficient operations, which imperiled the safety of workers and cargo. The operations manager believed that several accidents could be traced to the CEO overruling him and demanding more strenuous work schedules. "Some guys can always be bribed with a small bonus," he said. The manager also thinks that several acts of sabotage (such as limestone in the tank), requiring costly repairs, are related to the frustration felt by the truckers.

Clearly, the scientific approach to task separation unleashed a huge increase in the productive powers of labor. Division of tasks allows vastly more efficient manufacture, transportation, medical care, and government administration. For better or worse, it makes the large organization possible.

But there is a human cost to the separation of tasks. Early on, Karl Marx observed that the techniques of mass production dissociate or *alienate* workers from the end product. Emile Durkheim later incorporated this idea into his theory of *anomie*, conceived of as a far-reaching breakdown of social norms and bonds. Both thinkers noticed that modern industry conceptualizes human beings as production and cost factors, analogous to machines or real estate. Miller and Form state that the industrial mindset imagines the worker as a "biological machine."[46] As the industrial era developed, machines were no longer thought of as tools that supported human work; rather, workers were regarded—and treated—as part of the machinery that kept the company operating. An employee who was injured or incapacitated, even in the line of duty, was discarded and replaced like a broken piece of equipment.

The production line mindset was an unanticipated consequence of the separation of tasks. Thanks to labor unions and government regulation, some of the harsher features of the factory system have been mitigated, but it is naïve to think that the mindset itself is passé and that modern team methods have taken over. *Working* is in large measure a study of the production line system, in which work becomes a series of "daily humiliations" endured by both blue- and white-collar employees.[47] "I'm a machine," says the spot welder. "I'm caged," says the bank teller. The model of labor as an extension of machines has been incorporated into the service industry as well. The so-called "electronic sweatshop" is the new version of the old strategy of compartmentalizing tasks and interactions to the point where the humanity and dignity of workers are ignored.

Labor economists and industrial designers of a century ago continue to set the tone and style of their disciplines. Consider the attitudes of Frederick Taylor, the father of modern personnel and industrial management. In his seminal work, *The Principles of Scientific Management*, Taylor performed time studies and other research into the capacity of laborers to perform various kinds of work and the proper division of tasks within a larger process. After

---

46 Delbert C. Miller and William H. Form, *Industrial Sociology: An introduction to the sociology of work* (New York: Harper & Brothers, 1951). Interestingly, this image parallels the mindset of early modern medicine, which understood patients in mechanical terms as collections of body parts, or in plumbing terms as functioning homeostatic systems (Leder, 1997).

47 Studs Terkel, *Working: People Talk About What They Do All Day and How They Feel About What They Do* (New York: Pantheon Books, 1974).

observing men pick up 92-pound chunks of pig iron, carry them several yards, and then drop them in another place, he wrote, "This job is so crude and elementary in its nature that the writer firmly believes that it would be possible to train an intelligent gorilla so as to become a more efficient pig iron handler than any man can be." The workers deliberately kept a controlled and leisurely pace, handling about 12 tons per day. Sensing that he was dealing with laggards, Taylor set out to prove that workers could handle at least 46 tons per day:

> First, we carefully watched and studied about 75 men for several days, finally choosing four whom we deemed capable of handling the required tonnage. A careful study was then made of each of these men. We looked up their history as far back as practicable and thorough inquiries were made as to the character, habits, and ambition of each of them. After this selection we then chose to focus on the first, the man called Schmidt.
>
> Schmidt was called out from among the gang of pig iron handlers: "Schmidt, are you a high-priced man?"
>
> "Vell, I don't know vat you mean." [The conversation goes on for several minutes in this vein.]
>
> "Well, if you are a high-priced man, you will do exactly as this man tells you tomorrow, from morning until night. When he tells you to pick up a pig and walk, you pick it up and walk, and when he tells you to sit down and rest, you sit down. You do that straight through the day. And what's more, no back talk. Now, a high-priced man does just what he's told to do and no more back talk. Do you understand that?"
>
> Schmidt started to work, and all day long, and at regular intervals, was told by the man who stood over him with a watch. "Now pick up a pig and walk. Now sit down and rest. Now walk, now rest. . . . " He worked when he was told to

work, and rested when he was told to rest, and at half past five in the afternoon had his 47.5 tons loaded on the car. And he practically never failed to work at this pace and do the task that was set him during the three years I was at Bethlehem [Steel Company]."[48]

Modern time studies and quota management programs may not mock workers' accents the way Taylor does, but they still reify employees as machines to be controlled and regulated: work, rest, work, rest. Agencies like the Occupational Safety and Health Administration (OSHA) may have ameliorated some of the abuses of a century ago, but it is still common for managers to refuse to acknowledge workers as truly human. The point of this observation is not to criticize with hindsight the mindset of the industrial world of 1900. It is to discover the root causes of a mindset that is still prevalent today.

The production line mindset has two important side effects. First, employees are not given a sense of the organization's mission, nor are they thought to need any sense of a larger purpose. Doing only part of a job over and over again is not in itself a denigration of dignity; collaboration and specialization can be an opportunity for growth and accomplishment for all concerned. But preventing employees, deliberately or not, from having a holistic picture of the process or sharing in the end product relegates them to being a means to an end. The sharing of goals and rewards is crucial to dignified relationships in organizations. When workers are instructed only to do a job and are not informed about the strategic purpose of their effort, misjudgments are made and substitute goals quickly take over.

> In the service economy of today, the production line mindset extends to seeing clients (customers or patients) as pure commodities. In April 1998, the state of Florida started an investigation into the "dumping" of Medicaid patients by private nursing homes. "Many patients were crying, 'Where are we going to go?' They were treated like cattle being herded," said one witness.

---

48 Frederick Winslow Taylor, *The Principles of Scientific Management* (New York: Harper, 1911).

For example, in 1976, the city council of a Dutch town was confronted with an unexpected overtime request for twenty-five thousand guilders in the bookkeeping department. What had happened? An inquiry revealed that three accountants had spent months working overtime to trace a bookkeeping error of about three guilders. The city council responded to this embarrassing gaffe by implementing new regulations requiring management to describe the goals behind every task and to encourage workers to use their common sense in making judgments. The point was to create a more interactive, less passive work style in which the opinions of employees at every level were considered.

A Chicago attorney who was working temporarily as a legal secretary related a similar scenario. As an employee in a large law firm, she soon came to feel that "it was no longer important whether I had the ability to think beyond what I was told to do. I wasn't expected to reason a + b = c. I was just told to 'do a.' But I didn't know why I was doing 'a.' I wasn't told, and I wasn't encouraged to think about, what effect 'a' would have on the rest of the equation."[49]

These managerial attitudes show that Taylor's description of "cooperation from workers" still holds true in many organizations—employees are expected "to do what they are told to do promptly and without asking questions or making suggestions." It is dangerous for workers to think and express themselves too much in an organization that relies on the production line mindset, because thinking and expressing are understood as obstacles to efficiency. Good machines don't reflect or interact; they just hum. It follows that employee-cogs, as subsets of the machine, should be treated only in the context of the machine system. In machine-oriented factory work, machines and humans are simply replaced with other machines and humans when they break down or are injured. In a service organization, the employee who performs the work is considered a part, not a person. The demand for a robot-like execution of commands denies workers the right to express thoughts and emotions. In many situations, workers are positively evaluated for jettisoning all emotion and human sympathy in the name of "professionalism."

---

[49] Personal interview.

A second effect of the production line mindset is the fear-based relationship between supervisors and subordinates. When workers are treated as units of labor, their behavior is understood in terms of compliance, not commitment. Compliance is fueled by a variety of fears: fear of losing income or face, or fear of failure, or of the unknown. Fear moves quickly through a compliance-oriented organization. While a CEO may not enjoy motivating through fear, it is an inevitable corollary of viewing people as fungible cost factors. This humanity-denying perception leads to a fear-infused corporate culture in which indignity and abuse become tools to enforce compliance. As one study notes:

> Corporate abuse has many faces. In its most obvious form it includes discrimination, harassment, systematic humiliation, arbitrary dismissals, demotions without cause, arbitrary withholding of resources, and financial manipulation. Its more subtle manifestations include lack of support, penny-pinching, micro-management, constant inadequate miscommunication, hidden agendas, oppressive surveillance, inverted priorities, and smothering corporate cultures.[50]

The production line mindset does not consider the motivations of the individual worker relevant or significant. It fails to recognize the potential gains from connecting individual efforts and goals with corporate purposes. It also fails to understand that a disconnect will eventually undermine the competitiveness of the organization as personnel turnover and its associated costs increase.

Tackling the production line mindset will be easier in the future, as the knowledge worker becomes more prevalent. However, many corporate cultures continue to embrace Taylor's century-old assumptions. Despite some progress, management still must strive to liberate itself from the ideas of the past.

---

[50] Lesley Wright and Marti D. Smye, *Corporate Abuse: How "lean and mean" robs people and profits* (New York: MacMillan Publishing Company, 1996).

The Military Mindset (Privates in Boot Camp)

The screenwriters for the popular TV program *ER* spent months in large urban hospital emergency rooms. The exposure allowed them to capture the interpersonal dynamics that come into play when life hangs in the balance and fast teamwork is essential. The program's camerawork captures the fast, aggressive, purposeful behavior of the players. *ER* provides a peek into a world of highly trained professionals who can operate as a well-oiled machine and mostly put their personality differences aside in moments of crisis. The writers of *ER* have also effectively dramatized the tension between the hospital's legal and bureaucratic requirements and the doctors' own life-saving instincts.

Many people's jobs center on emergency situations, including firefighters, police officers, prison guards, Red Cross and Federal Emergency Management Agency workers, insurance claims adjusters and, especially, the armed forces. Many more workers have jobs that periodically create their own "emergencies." Journalists, for example, work against deadlines; anyone who has ever been in a newsroom knows the daily rhythm of frantic activity and recovery. Tax lawyers and accountants work feverishly in March and April, driven by the IRS deadline of midnight, April 15. Postal workers can expect overtime assignments every year on the 15th of April and before Christmas. Farmers and truckers can experience very long work weeks when weather or markets offer sudden opportunities.

Violent Reactions To Boot Camp Tactics

In December 1997, a big brouhaha erupted in the NBA, after basketball player Latrell Sprewell apparently tried to strangle his coach, P. J. Carlesimo, twice. The NBA Players Association supported Sprewell in his fight against the penalties set by NBA Commissioner David Stern. The players stood behind their peer, because his outbursts were understood as reactions to the traumatizing behavior of the coach, who is known for his abusive leadership style.

In an emergency, employees work in a pressure-filled environment. Surprisingly, these situations often result in positive work experiences. Workers know what the stakes are and perform at a high level despite fatigue and stress. Suppressed leadership qualities surface, and team operations take on a smoothness that makes people wonder, to quote an interview, "Why can't we do this all the time?"

Basic training and boot camp can be beneficial for young men. Witness the reflections of Warren Brookson, college athlete and army reserve member.

> I needed a break, to get my head focused again on what I wanted to do. I learned patience, humility, how to look at a situation and get through it. . . . I learned modesty.
>
> My experience in the army taught me to play under control and suppress the kind of outbursts that negated my game when I was younger.
>
> The army helped me to keep my emotions locked up and control my temper, because I can't afford to have a temper.[51]

The military mindset follows from the positive expectations that many people have about intense training and education. It assumes that boot camp builds character, that detoxification programs for drug addicts should use the "cold turkey" method, and that super-intense training methods are the right way to secure a "win." We let trainers and coaches in boot camps, army barracks, sport clubs, and medical schools get away with enormous amounts of abusive behavior, because we accept the idea that soldiers, athletes, and doctors need to be forcefully, even violently, molded into effective team players. In boot camp, there is a concerted effort to break down the uniqueness of the individual. Trainees are deliberately overworked and deliberately humiliated. They are forced to march long distances, perform trivial chores, and go long stretches with little or no sleep. Above all, they are not allowed to express an opinion to superiors except in a hyper-respectful manner, a courtesy that is deliberately unreciprocated. Many medical schools and other training programs subject their

---

[51] *Chicago Tribune*, March 7, 1998.

students and resident MDs to abusive practices that have similarities to those used by the military.[52] The motto: Be superior, or be out.

In the army barracks, fire or police academy, and, to some extent, the medical school, such tactics have legitimate ends. In emergency situations, when the adrenaline is rushing, individuals *must* move quickly and react as a unit. This can only be accomplished if each team member has acquired habits of obedience and self-sacrifice. Good teamwork and positive results in the face of adversity are exhilarating, and team members often acknowledge its benefit.

However, no matter how often business executives refer to Patton or *The Art of War*, companies are not in a combat zone. The excitement of emergency, high-risk operations cannot be sustained for long periods, and cannot become the norm for employees. No organization can survive solely on tactics based on the military mindset. No person can permanently deny himself or herself for the greater good of the organization. That attitude belongs to the era of serfs and lords or slaves and masters. Yet, the military mindset is curiously dominant throughout many corporations. In the 1930s, James Mooney and Alan Reilly promoted the military model as one of the best ways of organizing industries. Around the same time, Chester Barnard developed the notion that industrial workers have a zone of indifference, allowing managers to get away with some level of abuse without repercussions.[53] This mindset has

> Wall Street glorifies the ruthlessness of the boot camp mindset, as embodied in executives such as Al Dunlap, known *admiringly* as "Chainsaw Al." When Dunlap was hired to lead Sunbeam, the price of its stock rose spectacularly. He proceeded to gut the company in the name of shareholder value. Only when it became clear in the summer of 1998 that Sunbeam's financial reports were "unconventional" did he get the boot. Ruthless CEO's can become so obsessive that they can bring down whole corporations. Witness the Continental Airline saga of the early 1990s, as well as the last years of Henry Ford.

52 Debra L. Klamen, Linda S. Grossman, and David Kopacz, "Posttraumatic Stress Disorder Symptoms in Residents Physicians Related to Their Internship," *Academic Psychiatry* 19, no.3 (1995): 142-49.

53 James D. Mooney and Alan C. Reilly, *The Principles of Organization* (New York: Harper & Bros., 1939); Barnard, 1956.

endured into the present, where the free market is portrayed as a literal battleground, and where modern-day Social Darwinists control the ideologies of the business schools.

For example, in an article titled "Business as War," the *Wall Street Journal* profiled the CEO of Cabletron Systems, Inc. At the end of one obscenity-laced "pep talk" to new recruits, he held up a beach ball inscribed with the name of Cabletron's archrival, then plunged a huge combat knife into the ball, as the crowd cheered. This warlike method of rallying the troops was apparently typical at Cabletron, where the environment was compared to that of a pirate ship. "If you were in the gang," one employee said, "you got rich. If you weren't, you walked the plank." Adrenaline and testosterone flowed, but the price of working at Cabletron was high. One salesman was fired in front of his colleagues for being thirty minutes late to a training session. Telephone-sales operations were a high-pressure affair. Once a set target of calls per hour was met, new and stricter targets were created. Managers fired a certain percentage of telemarketers without warning so that uncertainty about the future would keep employee motivation high. According to one salesperson, "The prevailing philosophy was management by fear and intimidation."[54] Teamwork and trust cannot last in such a corporate environment without strong-arm tactics.

The militant atmosphere of Cabletron and similar organizations is actually more exhausting and dehumanizing than real wars or emergency rooms. Such companies don't allow downtime and don't create periods of "peace" for employees to recover their sense of individual identity and worth, needs that have been curbed during periods of high stress and total team identification. Wright and Smye call management by fear and intimidation *deliberate abuse*: "A premeditated policy or strategy developed and executed on the wrongheaded assumption that it will get results by forcing workers to toe the line constantly."

---

54 John R. Wilke, "Business as War: 'Corporate Misfits' Who Run Cabletron Play a Rough Game – They Exhort Staff to Battle, Fire Freely, Go All-Out To Please the Customer – No Chairs in Meeting Rooms," *The Wall Street Journal*, April 9, 1993.

They tell the story of one retail company president who was dubbed "Godzilla" by his employees:

> He specialized in humiliating his staff in public and was universally feared and hated for his blistering criticism. His administrative assistant had a nervous breakdown and one of the buyers had a car accident when he was driving home in shock after a particularly bad attack of Godzilla's wrath. Godzilla kept close tabs on all of his staff, who were so afraid of spies in their midst that it was very difficult for co-workers to trust one another. When one employee commented that the pressures of her job had contributed to the breakdown of her marriage, Godzilla remarked, "Well, that means you can spend more time at work."[55]

The military mindset, which projects all situations as emergency or war situations, is, for most organizations, out of step with reality. In special circumstances, this mindset can be very efficient. But deliberate humiliation is not an effective long-term motivational strategy; it always backfires eventually. The military mindset disregards the dignity of workers and management, encourages abuse, and ignores the wholeness and uniqueness of each worker. When the boot camp approach is temporarily necessary, management must provide extra compensation for lost dignity, above and beyond the usual methods of paying overtime and bonuses.

The Social Science Mindset (Lab Rats of the Social Scientist)

Americans believe deeply in science and seek truth in numbers. J. L. Moreno wrote in the 1920s, "More than any other living variety of human species, the American man loves to express [status] in figures, he is the *homo metrum*." The

---

[55] Wright and Smye, 1996.

impact of that belief has been huge.[56] Scientific research has been institutionalized; all Western economies set aside a certain percentage of their revenue to fund basic research. It was Americans who first systematically coupled research with development, thereby making research the growth engine of our economy.

Not all science is treated equally, however. One of the great divides in the academic universe is between *hard* and *soft* science, referring to the relative strength of the inferences that can be drawn from the research findings. In the United States, the deep belief in the value of scientific data leads to a strong preference for the "hard" physical sciences and lesser support for "soft" social science research. Social sciences are much younger (Benjamin Franklin, for example, did not consider social phenomena legitimate topics of study), and they have a less rigid methodology regarding inferences. Nevertheless, this century has witnessed an enormous boom in social research, which has produced an extensive body of knowledge regarding human behavior, especially within organizations. Our understanding of motivation, rewards, direction, communication, and so on has increased greatly in recent decades.

Many managers today are eager to learn of the latest findings and theories of social scientists, but are reluctant to implement these theories with scientific rigor and consistency. Among the reasons for this reluctance, four factors stand out:

- Producing real change involves examining such sensitive issues as the organizational power structure, the wage structure, group dynamics, communication, and so on.
- Organizational obsession with the bottom line leads managers to seek shortcuts, neglect quality and service, and pay insufficient attention to process and detail.

---

56 One minor example of Americans' love of numbers is the extensive use of statistics by sports announcers and commentators. During the 1994 World Cup soccer championship, held in the United States, foreign reporters were exposed to data they had never collected before, which streamlined their analyses of the games. It led to a redefinition of the art of sports reporting.

- Managers rarely feel sufficiently secure in their identity to let their own performance, feelings, and ethics be subjected to scientific inquiry.
- People are generally resistant to radically new ideas. New approaches are most likely to gain wide acceptance if they depart only in small ways from existing beliefs and values.[57]

This unwillingness to rock the boat means a lack of reflection and a resistance to substantive change. It also leads to a selective reading of research findings, as managers seek social science nostrums that can be tested on the broader workforce while sparing the corporate elite from similar meddling. Adopting managerial techniques to alter the behavior of others, without seeking greater understanding of the system as a whole, is nothing more than manipulation of underlings. Consider the language used in the following excerpts from an essay titled "Behavior Modification on the Bottom Line":

> A very wise man once said, "It's not so much that people mind changing, it's that they mind being changed."

> Someone who expects to influence behavior must be able to manipulate the consequences of behavior. Whether managers realize it or not, they constantly shape the behavior of their subordinates by the way they utilize the rewards at their disposal. . . . A primary reason managers fail to "motivate" workers to perform in a desired manner is their failure to understand the power of the contingencies of reinforcement over their employee. . . . Conditioning is the process by which behavior is modified through manipulation of the contingencies of behavior . . . the differences among

---

57 Marion Pirie, "Women and the Illness Role: Rethinking Feminist Theory," *La Revue Canadienne de Sociologie et D'Anthropologie/The Canadian Review of Sociology & Anthropology* 25, no. 4 (1988): 628-48.

> these kind of contingencies depend on the consequences that result from the behavioral act. Positive reinforcement and avoidance learning are methods of strengthening desired behavior, while extinction and punishment are methods of weakening undesired behavior.[58]

The author seems to be talking about guinea pigs, not human beings.

Peters' and Waterman's *In Search of Excellence* is a detailed study of how to motivate workers and bring out the best in them. Their text has been very popular because of the prevailing lab rat mindset in Western managerial circles.[59] In response, Hugh Willmott wrote "When Weakness is Strength and Slavery is Freedom," a stinging rebuke to this type of personnel quality improvement blueprint.[60] Willmott argues that the manipulative nature of most quality improvement and motivational programs is deeply denigrating, in that it reduces the workforce to a mindless, faceless herd, and the individual worker to a series of variables. In such situations, the attention given to the worker, however well-intended, is ephemeral and insincere. Enhancing worker dignity is rarely a goal of such programs. What counts is the potential for bigger bottom lines and smoother work practices that make for fewer managerial headaches. Literature from labor studies

> Office cubicles—sometimes dubbed "veal pens" by workers—are very popular with management. Sales were at $3.4 billion in 1996. Lighting maker Bio-Brite tried to get into this market by introducing an artificial electric "window" that hangs on the wall like a picture. Focus groups had identified the lack of windows and spatial movement as major cubicle flaws. Whether the "window" will lead to higher productivity or more pen-induced stress was not studied.

58 W. Clay Hamner and Ellen Hamner, "Behavior Modification on the Bottom Line," *Organizational Dynamics* 4, no. 4 (1976): 2-21.

59 T. J. Peters and R. H. Waterman, Jr., *In Search of Excellence: Lessons from America's Best-Run Companies* (New York: Harper & Row, 1982).

60 Hugh Willmott, "When Strength is Ignorance, Slavery is Freedom: Managing Culture in Modern Organizations," *Journal of Management Studies* 30, no. 4 (1993): 515-52.

indicates that most workers are well aware of the fact that they serve as "scientific toys" for management when new programs are introduced and "volunteers" are sought. They understand that most of these programs are innately denigrating, driven by cost/benefit calculations and a lab rat view of individual employees.

Manipulation of employees based on a skimming of sociological or psychological findings can have dire consequences, potentially unleashing suppressed emotions and conflicts at a deep psychological level. Like the sorcerer's apprentice who went beyond his capabilities and unleashed chaos, managers may attempt to wield power beyond their understanding and control. Too often, supervisors use the techniques of behavior modification in oversimplified, underdeveloped form, resulting in unintended and often harmful consequences. The last decade has seen an increase in work-related homicides, which can be linked in part to the detrimental side effects of modern manipulation techniques.[61]

Distinguishing between positive and negative manipulation is not always easy. In the ideal organization, all persons work toward common, well-defined, and clearly understood goals and are given the means to actually achieve them; supervisors involve people openly in the achievement of those goals because they assume that employees are basically competent and reasonable. Green and Pawlak note in *Ethics and Manipulation in Organizations* that the ability to influence the behavior of others is essential in steering organizations and workers toward common goals. When influence is exerted on others *without their knowledge or consent*, it is negative manipulation, a violation of democratic norms.[62] When influence is open, interactive, and respectful of human dignity, then it may be considered positive manipulation. When workers are kept in the dark or are told to "just follow instructions," they lose connectedness and become alienated, distrustful, and apathetic. People are not lab rats.

---

61 Duncan Chappell and Vittorio Di Martino, *Violence at Work* (Geneva: ILO Publications, 1998).

62 But negative manipulation remains an important tool in many corporate cultures: Witness the popularity of Machiavelli's *The Prince* in boardrooms and business schools. Few leaders are willing to relinquish entirely the techniques described in that Renaissance manual of realpolitik.

When they sense they are being used for unknown, unshared ends, they naturally resist, either actively or passively.

The Psychological Roots of Abusive Behavior

While much workplace abuse is grounded in culture and mindset, some abuse is personal and psychological in origin, the product of rogue managers who operate outside of organizational norms. These bosses, usually at the middle management level, feel compelled to express their authority in hurtful ways. Their psychological insecurities and compensating strategies turn them into power-obsessed "Little Napoleons," who relish insulting and humiliating staff members, leading to simmering anger and frustration. The Freudian term for this problem is the "phallic-agentive syndrome." The term describes the mentality of those who compulsively abuse power and position. Over time, employee resentment of such treatment may dull, but only after employees have disengaged emotionally from their work.

What makes it possible for power abusers to rise within organizations? Part of the problem is that organizational recruitment processes and performance assessment procedures tend to focus on a handful of tangible accomplishments and skills. In such a system, bosses can get away with a wide range of behaviors not included in the evaluation checklist. (By the same token, positive, dignifying actions and attitudes often go unrecognized and unrewarded.) Eventually, the abusive boss becomes entrenched in the hierarchy and the abusive behavior becomes institutionally sanctioned.

Toward a Dignifying Mindset

In addition to the four mindsets discussed here, others are apparent in the work world, each with its own effects on the dignity of other members of the organization. The teamwork (one-of-the-gang) mindset reveals the tension between the organizational reality of hierarchy and the human need for camaraderie. A "one-of-the-gang" supervisor or executive attempts to motivate people by appearing to disregard hierarchical boundaries and act like a peer to subordinates, rather than a stereotypical boss. In its normal, functional, and benign form, this mindset is part and parcel of the informal American work and service culture. It is exemplified by the senior executive who tells employees to "Just call me Bill" and by nurses who address elderly patients by their first names. This mindset has proliferated, especially in the Silicon Valley, with the increase in the number of highly skilled technicians and knowledge workers.

When the teamwork mindset is used to soften rank differences and to underscore the value of workers as team members, but not to deny the existence of hierarchy, then it may very well help the organization.

There are, however, many instances of supervisors pressing too hard for acceptance, thereby losing the respect of their underlings. When a CEO "moons" a group of employees at a poolside company sales meeting, the result is embarrassment, not acceptance.[63] The one-of-the-gang culture can also lead to group transgressions of social norms, or mob behavior, as leaders refuse to set the moral tone. A large Japanese company, for instance, organized parties for managers at nude dancing clubs with prostitutes, while Navy fliers once molested women annually at the notorious Tailhook Association conventions. The "camaraderie" generated in these settings has nothing to do with collegiality and mutual respect; they were cults of self and group debasement. When such one-of-the-gang displays occur, employees don't feel empowered, recognized, or dignified. They feel compromised, and lose respect, and trust, qualities that enable the organization to work effectively. Organizational rank is not in itself a violation of dignity. Leaders who establish themselves as first among equals dignify the whole team. The popularity of mentor relationships shows that people need and desire established role models on which to pattern their own behavior.

The dehumanization of employees and others by destructive organizational mindsets is a pervasive problem. The destructive mindsets described above are both an ethical and an economic problem for organizations. It is necessary to find alternative models that are truly transformative, yet realistic and cost-effective, models that help managers learn the real meaning of dignifying others.

---

63 Personal observation.

Chapter Four

The Prevalence of Denigration

I had based my life on a myth. I believed that the American Dream was for everyone, regardless of race, even in Corporate America. I believed it when the men of Texaco repeatedly assured me that they really meant what they said in their glossy recruiting brochures. They welcomed diversity; it made good business sense; it was merit, not color, that counted.

I kept my side of the bargain by working as hard and productively as any white man, but the rewards Texaco promised for me did not come. Despite consistently high ratings for my performance, I was denied opportunity after productively because of my race. The last straw came when, after a promotion I wanted was given to a white man with lesser qualifications, my bosses actually expected me to train him.

What happened to me is a story that Texaco never wanted you to know. In fact the company did everything it could to try to stop me from telling it, including forcing my resignation. But this story is too important to keep it all to myself; I must share it.

—Excerpted from *Roberts vs. Texaco: A True Story of Race and Corporate America*[64]

In 1996, after tapes were discovered revealing how Texaco executives planned to destroy damaging documents relating to a discrimination lawsuit lodged by African-American employees, Texaco settled for $176 million. During the settlement proceedings, a Texaco attorney told the group of plaintiffs that "Texaco will never,

---

64 Bari-Ellen Roberts and Jack E. White, *Roberts vs. Texaco: A True Story of Race and Corporate America* (New York: Avon Books, 1998).

ever throw a bunch of money at a bunch of blacks. You all can forget that."[65] Although the court did not order the corporation to change its attitudes about race, Texaco agreed to establish a diversity program, overseen by an independent task force. Roberts, who now leads the African-American Association for Corporate Responsibility, concludes that "the workplace is the battleground as the fight for civil rights braces for the millennium."[66]

Blatant Denigration

What we now consider to be blatant racism and sexism was mainstream thinking when the United States was established. Indeed, we can consider it progress that blatant manifestations of racism, as at Texaco, are now legally and socially unacceptable. Federal law has established what may be considered a maximum legal level of indignity. Because of the threat of litigation, it makes financial sense for management to offer employees "diversity training" and to enforce rules about insensitive behavior.

These actions, while salutary, do not eliminate the social costs of sexism and racism. As in John Adams' time, white men still largely define the context of women's and minorities' struggles for emancipation, forcing them to waste energy on defensive arguments and to channel their thinking into narrow issues of race, ethnicity, and gender.[67]

> The psychological effects of this institutionalized sexism are captured by this headline: *"At What Age Does a Girl Dream of Becoming President? At What Age Does She Decide it's Impossible?"*
>
> (From the White House Project of the American Association of University Women.)

Sexism and racism are not the only forms of group indignity. Social denigration by caste or class has very old roots as well. In

---

65 Carol Memmott, "Author offers ugly account of Texaco lawsuit," *USA Today*, p. 6B, April 3, 1998.

66 Ibid.

67 Stephen L. Carter, *Reflections of an Affirmative Action Baby* (New York: Basic Books, 1991).

American society, this form of denigration has now befallen the impoverished class known as the homeless. Newspapers report that homeless people are used in illegal asbestos-removal scams, where they are employed in this extremely dangerous and delicate work without adequate protection and training. Attorney General Janet Reno expressed outrage, stating, "This is shameful human exploitation. Knowingly removing asbestos improperly is criminal, and using vulnerable people for such activity violates the basic standard of human decency."[68] Making outcasts of social groups, a characteristic of fascist regimes, has no place in a democracy, which is premised on the idea that all people matter.

Many people experience subtle racism and subtle sexism, which are harder to describe and document than the blatant varieties, but are just as harmful over time. Wilhelmina Essed describes how this "everyday racism" is expressed through tone, word choice, and body language. Essed explains how these subtly hostile behaviors engender a defensive, negative attitude that leaves victims drained and paralyzed.[69] Van Dijk examines the racist premises that underlie many everyday English phrases.[70] Other writers, such as Frankenberg, have recently begun discussing the concept of "whiteness" as an expression of majority ideology.[71]

"Glass ceilings" are often perceived as expressions of institutionalized sexism or racism. The picture gallery of the CEOs of the Fortune 500 companies, which is published every year, is indicative of these ceilings. In 1996, there were two women and one black person among the five hundred mug shots.

Many members of minority groups have to work and produce in environments marked by the presence of everyday bigotry and

---

68 "Wisconsin Men Charged in Asbestos Removal," *The New York Times*, p. A16, April 25, 1998.

69 Philomena Essed, *Understanding Everyday Racism: An Interdisciplinary Theory* (Newbury Park, CA: Sage Publications, 1991).

70 Teun A. van Dijk, *Elite Discourse and Racism* (Newbury Park, CA: Sage Publications, 1993).

71 Ruth Frankenberg, *White Women, Race Matters: The social construction of whiteness* (Minneapolis: University of Minnesota Press, 1994).

sexism. Biases can be so deeply embedded that the insulter may not be aware of his or her prejudices and attitudes, and may be genuinely surprised if others take offense. The great advantage of subtle insults is that they are more deniable than blatant ones.

"Peter," an MD and a university dean, is a gentle man raised in an upper-class European milieu. He has run several departments over the course of his career and been involved with many large-scale research projects. In his twenty-five years of hiring professionals to help conduct research, he has never hired a female researcher. In the few cases where he collaborated with women researchers, his name always appeared before theirs in the papers. When confronted with these observations, he was flabbergasted. He was unaware of his own bias. He insisted that people had been reading him all wrong and that this was just a statistical fluke. He also vowed that he would prove his colleagues wrong. The future will tell, but his response indicated an attitudinal flexibility that bodes well for minimizing the denigration of dignity.

The battles to erase racism and sexism are a very important part of the larger effort to create a climate in which dignity can be pursued. It makes no sense for managers to address interpersonal issues of dignity and respect if the larger issues of gender, race, and ethnicity are ignored. Thus, the South Carolina military college known as The Citadel must address at the institutional level the question of recruiting women and persons of color before its faculty can dignify women or minorities on a personal level. Honor presumes dignity; The Citadel thrives on honor. To use another example, Texaco's sponsorship of artists and other goodwill gestures seem hollow in light of the class-action suit claiming that discrimination at Texaco was systematic. If denigration of entire groups is tolerated, it makes little sense to fuss over the personal worth of an individual. With that fundamental proviso in mind, this chapter will examine categories and examples of personal denigration.

Avoidance

It is normal to feel unease when interacting with someone who is in mourning or experiencing a personal or professional crisis. Many workers who are grieving have suffered accidents, or who were laid off report avoidance behavior on the part of their peers. Folger and Skarlicki describe the process of avoidance by supervisors as "managerial distancing," when tough times make for tough bosses.[72] During periods of downsizing, managers and colleagues who were not affected tend to withdraw from social interaction with the victims, creating social distance. When difficult decisions that will hurt some workers have to be implemented, many managers try to transfer the blame. Unable to deal with face-to-face communications, many managers resort to the psychological distance of e-mail, departmental memos, or letters, often delivered late Friday afternoon.

Delivering bad news such as layoffs, reprimands, or demotions is a fact of organizational life. It is never a pleasant experience, but managers display a dignifying attitude when they communicate that news personally and face to face. In one university department, faculty received e-mail notification of their salary increases or lack thereof. One message read, "You will not receive any salary increase this year or in the future." Such treatment creates an emotional and social distance, since the professor in question can accept the content of the decision, but is troubled by the insultingly impersonal way in which it was delivered. The same department head confused the issue even more the next week by sending the same professor an e-mail telling him that he had been named as interim department head during the chief's three-week trip abroad. The department head then left that same evening without talking to the professor, informing him of coming events, or in any way preparing him for the responsibilities so ineptly delegated.

Avoidance behavior is common among managers and leaders confronted with potentially emotional situations. Many managers dread giving annual or semi-annual performance reviews. Managers often receive copious training in the fine art of performance evaluation. The emphasis is usually on technique and communication style. But the core challenge that makes evaluations so difficult—the need for a dignifying context—is avoided. Managers, looking up the

---

72 Robert Folger and Daniel P. Skarlicki, "When Tough Times make for Tough Bosses: Managerial Distancing as a Function of Layoff Blame," *Academy of Management Journal* 48, no. 1 (1998): 79-87.

ladder to the next promotion, often talk themselves out of close relationships with subordinates. They are fully aware that the performance of the workers they are reviewing depends in large part on the quality of their own leadership. When the dignity of the worker is not acknowledged, the performance evaluation process becomes a grand search for the "high average" or similar safe non-classifications. With dignity part of the equation, the evaluation exercise can energize employees to fulfill organizational as well as personal goals.

> Formalized evaluations often contain very little pertinent information since the contents have to be shared with the evaluated worker. Often, managers add personal notes to the forms that are sent to the human resources department. Somebody within the federal government has compiled a number of these notes and put them on the Internet. Here are some examples from the Military Officer Efficiency Reports:
>
> - Works well when under constant supervision and cornered like a rat in a trap.
> - I would not allow this employee to breed.
> - His men would follow him anywhere, but only out of morbid curiosity.
> - If you give him a penny for his thoughts, you'll get change.
> - If you stand close enough to him, you can hear the ocean.
> - If brains were taxed, he would get a rebate.
>
> While often humorous, these notes also indicate a degree of cowardly behavior vis-à-vis the worker. (From http://miljokes.com/a/may03/090503.htm)

Avoidance generally accompanies the cognitive process of rationalization. When regrouping occurs after downsizing, blaming victims on the work floor serves to justify and excuse the feelings of relief among the survivors. Insult is added to injury as workers fail to acknowledge the hurt that follows a loss of social ties and are unwilling to invest in empathy.

People are increasingly wary about committing themselves too strongly to their peers on the work floor, deliberately weakening their ties to co-workers because they are afraid of the potential for hurt. The workers who don't get fired may feel sorry for their unlucky colleagues, but they tend to do little in terms of outreach.

The sense of loss, loneliness, and shame associated with unemployment is well documented by social scientists. Interestingly, retirees don't experience this stigma. Thus, it is *how* one leaves work, not the leaving itself, that counts. Temporary workers, who make up a substantial part of the U.S. workforce, also experience avoidance behavior, further emphasizing their marginality.

The social consequences of avoidance behavior are significant but hard to measure. Stress levels are much higher among workers perceived as different, such as minorities, gays, and employees who are handicapped or obese. Labor law tries to remedy some of the blatant abuses, but has not produced full redress. Attitudes don't change quickly or easily, and some types of avoidance behavior are socially acceptable. For instance, when a driver stops on the highway to help others in distress (an incidence of admirable non-avoidance) he is likely to be cursed out by other motorists who have to slow down to pass his standing vehicle. How much easier, in such a climate, to just barrel along in our own bubble worlds and let the professionals deal with problems!

Avoidance behavior sanctioned by authority can be even worse than peer avoidance. The extensive violence, vandalism, and loss of productivity caused by disgruntled workers could be greatly reduced if workers' dignity was a central theme in organizational behavior. Buried in many police accounts of workers who turned violent are episodes of denigration of dignity and the experience of workplace isolation. Avoidance and other forms of social distancing can lead to a powerful backlash.

Disgruntled employees who explode violently are often socially isolated.[73] An act of social distancing can then trigger unforeseen reactions. In Allentown, Pennsylvania, for instance, a worker at a food-service plant was sent home for disciplinary reasons. He returned one hour later, confronted the supervisors, shot three of them, and then killed himself.[74]

---

73 Raymond B. Flannery, *Violence in the Workplace* (New York: Crossroad Publishers, 1995).

74 Associated Press, June 5, 1998.

Avoidance and social distancing are products of the bureaucratic mindset, with its assumption of purely "rational" decision-making based on impersonal relations. The individual's need for empathy and social integration is denied and even ridiculed in such a context, and tough bosses become inhumane bosses. By acting out the natural tendency for avoidance within the harsh context of an impersonal bureaucratic mindset, we create the potential for disaster.

Making Enemies of Employees I: Handling Collective Conflict

A different kind of avoidance by management occurs when workers change from "us" to "them." People who were part of the team can suddenly become outsiders and outcasts. During strikes, it becomes very difficult to dignify the opposing party. Denigrating actions and harsh words can turn negotiable differences into all-out conflict, offending the sense of dignity in both camps. In democracies, strikes are considered a legitimate labor tactic in most sectors of the economy. However, legalizing strikes is not the same thing as defusing the emotions stirred by them. Thus, the International Labor Organization, the AFL-CIO, and other labor organizations spend large amounts of time and energy in discussing the "etiquette" of striking. In most member-countries of the Organization for Economic Cooperation and Development (OECD), the national employer organizations also develop guidelines and institute training sessions to respond to strikes in a positive manner.

> In Almelo, Holland, during a strike in 1963, one union member crossed the picket line daily, yet maintained good social relations with his striking colleagues. Upon inquiry, it turned out that he had petitioned the union for permission to work. The union obliged him because he had to feed fourteen children. The same worker was also the only one who was allowed by his colleagues to produce above quota. His rate-busting was needed to feed that big a family. The relevant point here is that he conferred with his peers *and* his bosses.

In the United States, however, large employers tend to favor a kind of war strategy. Hiring of replacement workers, a tactic that is very rare if not illegal in other nations, is a legitimate management tactic in the United States. This practice is extremely divisive, making a farce of the so-called "company commitment strategies" and other "enlightened" labor relations policies touted by executives. Striking workers see replacement workers as an assault not just on their livelihoods, but on their dignity and stake in the organization. In countries with strong social democratic traditions, "scabs" are considered scum and subject to extreme forms of avoidance.

The lockout is the managerial equivalent of the strike. During lockouts, the normal relationship between workers and the organization is severed. This painful process is based on deeply held beliefs that monetary investment trumps labor investment and institutional identification. In itself, however, a lockout is not denigrating; it does not deny the value or humanity of workers. When not executed carefully, however, lockouts can humiliate and exacerbate conflict, as illustrated by the following incident, which was related by an office worker:

> When the fire alarm went off, we weren't too concerned. It had happened before. "Just a drill," said the supervisor, "let's go." I grabbed my purse and headed for the exit, not bothering to take a coat, since we would be back in a few minutes.
>
> Outside, most of the several hundred workers stood in the grass, smoking and talking. After about ten minutes, the alarm went off and the folks headed back in. But the line at the main entrance wasn't moving fast at all. I wondered what was keeping us. Someone yelled, "What's going on?" After a while it became clear that they were checking names at the door. I was glad I had brought my purse and ID cards. I thought, "This security thing is getting out of hand." You know, our company was in the computer software business, and things had become pretty complex in the last several months.
>
> As we gradually approached the entrance, something was strange. There was a whole bunch of security guards standing around the head of human resources. She was holding a clipboard and directing each worker either into the

building or off to the side. I was asked to wait outside as well, although I had my ID card on me. It was cold and I regretted not having my coat. As I waited and the group grew bigger, I became annoyed and we were fussing about what was going on. Damned security, we thought.

After about twenty minutes, the HR person came with her security guards to our group. There were over a hundred of us. Delores got a megaphone from one of the guards and started to read: "Ladies and gentlemen, this is to inform you that, as of this moment, you are no longer employed by this company. All of you will receive the severance packages negotiated in your contracts. You will receive information in the mail concerning continuing coverage of your insurance benefits, as mandated by U.S. law. Any personal effects in your work area will be boxed and sent to you C.O.D. All photo IDs, voice mailboxes, and e-mail addresses are no longer valid."

We were shocked, and disbelief kept us silent for a moment. Then the guys became angry and started to shout, "You can't do this! I've got stuff on my desk that I need." They started to push towards the HR chief, who stepped behind the guards and went inside. The security guards formed a line and then some of them pulled guns! I was crying and totally out of it. The guard with the bullhorn yelled that he would have us all arrested if we did not get off the private property. I ran away, because I did not want to see the anger and hurt of my colleagues. In my car, I could hardly get the key in the ignition, my hands were shaking so much. How dare they do this? I had my medicine in my desk. I drove for hours before calming down. I felt so humiliated, like a dog kicked out of the house.

Later I became angry. Why did my boss not just call me to his office and explain the layoff? We were treated like cattle, to be selected for slaughter. Later some of my colleagues who were kept at the company called me a few times, but they

> didn't know what to say or do. Many of them are looking for other jobs; nobody trusts anybody anymore. But then again, the companies are all the same. One day they need you, next day they kick you out. What can you do? [75]

Enemies were created and self-confidence was shattered. The workers who stayed saw their motivation levels plummet and started looking for other jobs. In the year since the computer company pulled the fire-drill stunt, worker productivity has declined significantly and the company has not yet recouped its loss of market share.

Making Enemies of Employees II: Playing with Pay

In the summer of 1998, Allegheny University of Health Sciences asked the school's faculty and medical staff to accept a 25 percent pay cut after the school's parent institution, the Allegheny Health, Education, and Research Foundation, went bankrupt. The Board of Regents fired the CEO and five other top administrators for gross mismanagement. These six administrators had received and cashed in more than $8 million in stock options in March of that year. Funds earmarked for research and restricted medical endowments had been used to pay the system's mounting debt. Faculty and staff became outraged and disgusted with what they called thievery and unbecoming conduct, prompting criminal investigation.[76]

> In its April 20, 1998 issue, *Business Week* reported that the CEOs at 365 of the nation's largest companies received, on average, a 35 percent pay increase in 1997, bringing the average CEO salary to $7.8 million. This increase is ten times the national average pay raise for all workers (3.3 percent).

Pay is more than compensation; for many individuals, it is a gauge of individual worth. Employers must proceed cautiously when countering employees with pay expectations.

---

[75] Personal interview.

[76] Katherine Mangan, "Outrage and a Sense of Betrayal at Allegheny U. of Health Sciences," *Chronicle of Higher Education* A 49, September 18, 1998.

The average CEO of a major U.S. corporation made 42 times the average hourly worker's pay in 1980. By 1990 that figured had nearly doubled to 85 times. In 2000, the average CEO salary was 531 times that of the average hourly worker. This phenomenon reinforces the attitude that "employees of the organization are second-rate".[77] The stunning rise in CEO pay produced an image problem for industry during the 1990s.

But the problem goes beyond image. Employees feel denigrated because CEOs and boards of directors don't even understand the feelings of resentment, anger, and frustration that are generated. Anger, for example, at the insensitivity of AT&T Chairman Robert Allen when he sent a memo in 1996 to employees defending his $2.7 million salary, after he had just held a news briefing outlining a restructuring plan that would result in the layoff of forty thousand workers.[78] The denigration is underscored when these exorbitant executive incomes are paid in spite of poor performance by the organization.

Public awareness of the topic is having an effect, mostly through shareholder questions and subsequent action. In general, "the better CEOs . . . are sensitive to the relationship between their pay and their contribution and are sensitive to the fact that this information is public and will be communicated to

> Some schools of public health, agriculture, medicine, law, and business are set up as huge grant-writing shops, where faculty members are paid only if they bring in substantial outside funding. Managing in such competitive environments is very difficult. Faculty members in these pressure-cooker environments have been known to resort to stealing research ideas and protocols. Unhealthy competition eradicates mutual trust and the vigorous exchange of opinions. Mentoring becomes hollow and stress levels skyrocket when work becomes a Darwinian struggle for survival.

---

77 DeCenzo and Robbins, 1996.

78 Michael E. Kannell, "AT & T chief defends cutbacks, blasts media," *The Atlanta Journal and Constitution*, February 28, 1996.

79 Sallie L. Gaines, "Results often don't justify CEO pay," *Chicago Tribune*, April 10, 1998.

their employees."[79] Indeed, denigration can be ameliorated by such actions as freezing salaries, linking stock options to performance, and providing the same type of pay incentives to broader groups in the organization. Note should be taken of Roger A. Enrico, CEO of Pepsi Co, who in 1998 donated his annual base salary to fund scholarships for employees' children.[80]

Competition Ad Absurdum

Many companies base their motivational strategies on intense internal competition, willingly sacrificing cooperation and team-building efforts. In fact, companies often pursue contradictory agendas by pushing team concepts on the one hand and internal competition on the other. Of course, this serves only to confuse workers. Internal competition can be good for a company, when it is open, controlled, and fair. There is nothing wrong with having several workers compete for a promotion, lucrative assignment, or prestigious posting, as long as the competition is conducted honestly, and the criteria are reasonable and made known to all. Open competition between work teams is a key method of improving morale, tapping leadership skills, and adding some excitement and unpredictability to the work environment.

However, when internal competition pits workers against one another like gladiators in a Roman arena, everyone's dignity suffers:

> In a computer company that sells customized hardware and software, three units work with clients: the sales department, the installation department (which both installs hardware and software and trains customers to use the systems), and the after-sale technical maintenance department. The installation department relies on the strength of the sales group to get business. In 1997, headquarters, seeing sales slip, wanted to take cost-cutting action. The head of the installation department,

---

80 Carol Hymowitz, "IN THE LEAD: Does Rank Have Too Much Privilege? – Special Deals for Top Executives, While Underlings Lose Jobs and Savings, Are All Too Common," *The Wall Street Journal*, February 26, 2002.

husband of one of the vice-presidents, was promoted to another level in the company and a new head was recruited from within, on the condition that she fire seven of the eighteen installers.

In coordination with the legal team, the new department head decided to fire all installers, giving them one month's notice of their dismissal. The eighteen workers were encouraged to apply for their own positions. At the end of the month, they would learn whether they would stay or go. This was the first massive layoff in the company's history, and the rumor mill started spinning. Not only were the affected workers upset, but the whole workforce—over eighty people—felt their morale slip. These people were not naïve: they all knew the harsh realities of corporate life. But by firing them *en masse* and then asking them to *re-apply* for their old jobs, the company forced them to compete with one another for jobs in an organization where there would be no winners, only losers and survivors. The organizational social fabric was put to the test. They no longer knew how to work with each other, whom to trust, or what to work on. The whole organization was transformed into a non-productive beehive of gossip, as attention shifted from client needs to office politics.

When calm started to return, workers began reevaluating their investment in the company. Most applied for jobs elsewhere. Several sales managers quietly sold their shares. Several large customers canceled new orders, after being briefed by one of the fired employees, who was trying to set up shop independently. The shirking of responsibility and the creation of unnecessary hardship by one manager had a chilling effect on the work climate throughout the company. The affair will have serious long-term consequences for the company if headquarters is not willing to counteract the denigration by adopting new policies and attitudes and communicating the change to employees.[81]

---

81 Personal interview.

Competition is a valuable motivator. However, the winner-take-all approach to competition, with its many losers for every winner, is eventually destructive to the organization (as well as the larger society), leading to negative self-perceptions and demoralization.

Employees as Spare Parts: A question of control

In the early 1990s, news broke that twenty-five people died in a fire at a poultry processing plant in North Carolina. The shockingly high death toll occurred because the plant's fire escape doors were chain-locked. Plant managers (some of whom are still in jail as of this writing) wanted to control the whereabouts of the workers and eliminate the temptation to "sneak out for a smoke." When asked at trial why the company had not installed electronic alarm devices on the doors of the kind used in theaters, stores, and other large public buildings, a defendant claimed that "it was not cost-effective." This statement angered the jury, revealing the depth of indignity bestowed upon the mainly black, female workers.[82]

> Ms. Z., a teacher at an elementary public school, uses adult diapers, because she cannot leave her class of thirty-four children. Ms. M. has another solution: she has her whole class of twenty-two march together to the restrooms, where they wait in silence, holding hands.
>
> Mrs. C. was a meat packer. She and her co-workers were not allowed to leave their machines until a replacement was found. One day she had to use the bathroom and no replacement was available. Repeatedly, she asked the supervisor to replace her. He refused: as he saw it, his job was to control the work process, not to dignify the individual workers. Twice more he refused. When the replacement finally arrived, she found Mrs. C. in tears. The poor woman had soiled herself.

There is a widespread perception that management and leadership are a matter of *control.* But control without dignity, freedom, or spontaneity is a form of imprisonment, a

[82] Mark Mayfield, "In N.C., lingering pain, anger: Fatal fire fixed in memories," *USA Today*, p. 5A, March 11, 1992; Paul Leavitt, "N.C. plan owner gets 20 years in fire deaths," *USA Today*, p. 3A, September 15, 1992.

reduction of the human to the purely mechanical. We are thrilled by the graceful body control of great athletes like Michelle Kwan and Michael Jordan. When we see synchronized swimming or ballet, or the mass choreography at the start of the Olympic Games, we marvel at the complexity of controlled movement. However, the sight of soldiers goose-stepping appears sinister.

The dream of many managers who adhere to the philosophy of scientific management is to find workers of the same type, temperament, and skills, enabling managers to use these imaginary ant-like beings as spare parts for each other. The goal is to lead a huge chorusline of perfect bureaucratic efficiency, where all movements are smoothly choreographed and slip-ups are impossible. The spare-parts model underlies the staffing of police forces, the military, the nursing pool, and many organizations. For many years, temporary employment agencies advertised their services with this model in mind.

Control, like efficiency, is a necessary value within any organization, but it must be tempered by respect for the individual. Unfortunately, the concept is often stretched to the point of absurdity and destructiveness. In the sacred name of control, some managers deny the most basic human needs of employees. These abusive managers are locked into the spare-parts paradigm, in which employees are perceived not as people but as objects.

When control is too tight or is exercised in the wrong way or at the wrong time, it leads to denigration and employee reaction. Many years ago, the government passed laws requiring employers to install bathroom facilities for their workers. Denigration of employees needed to be ameliorated by official action. Amazingly, many employees still experience problems in this area; the Occupational Safety and Health Administration (OSHA) has cited numerous employers over the years for allowing filthy bathroom facilities. In such situations, workers often suppress the need to go to the bathroom by not drinking liquids for long periods, thereby increasing the risk of medical problems such as urinary tract infection.[83]

---

83 Marc Linder and Ingrid Nygaard, *Void Where Prohibited: Rest breaks and the right to urinate on company time* (Ithaca: ILR Press Cornell University, 1998).

It is a sad commentary on the state of worker dignity in the United States that in 1998, OSHA found it necessary to issue extra rulings that guaranteed workers not only the existence of washrooms in the workplace, but also the right and opportunity to use the facilities. According to OSHA officials, food-processing plants have the worst record in this regard, an observation that should make food consumers uneasy.

Currying Favor, Ratting, and Spying

A peculiar form of self-denigration occurs when workers approach senior executives and other VIPs in a servile manner that goes beyond respect. Most of us know people who routinely do something extra to ingratiate themselves with their superiors. The "something extra" is always directed at those who have some power. "Brownnosers" always seem to know the birthdays of the boss's children and their favorite hangouts.

Some people display this kind of behavior only on occasion. A contractor in Paramaribo, Suriname, who knew his trade and had a stable business, was very businesslike and straightforward during the implementation of a contract. However, when negotiating a contract, his demeanor was different. His body shrank, he avoided eye contact, and he pleaded and begged in an unctuous fashion. He lowered himself and denied his own pride and dignity to win the contract. Ironically, his attitude resulted in many lost contracts, because he never learned to become comfortable in negotiating; it remained the most difficult part of his job. An insecure man, he behaved at the negotiating table as though he had something to conceal.

Managers who participate in or encourage this type of behavior denigrate themselves as well. Workers know that most managers have significant ego investment in their career attainments, and therefore can be manipulated by flattery. Brownnosing does just that. For brownnosing to be successful, the boss must reward the behavior. In addition to being self-denigrating, brownnosing can potentially degrade a whole organization.

Ratting occurs when an employee informs his or her boss of facts or rumors about other workers. *Spying* consists of managerial tracking of employee behavior beyond socially accepted boundaries.

Ratting and spying are difficult to define; what an employee sees as spying, management may regard as diligent supervision. Many people feel insulted, not by the use of cameras themselves, but by the implication. The courts have rendered many decisions regarding the limits of workplace scrutiny. Installing cameras in restrooms and locker rooms is prohibited, as is secret tapping of customer-related telephone calls.

Some companies are establishing rules regarding the use of e-mail and the Internet on company computers. A few companies allow full and unfettered access to the Internet and e-mail. Others track every computer move their employees make. This is legal, as long as employees are aware of monitoring policies. However, when electronic tracking takes place in the absence of formal policies, it reduces employees to the status of children who must be watched at all times. Only designated officers of a company should police Internet usage. When lower-level managers spy, they denigrate themselves and eliminate the possibility of trust.

Dignity in Healthcare

Personal appearance helps convey our roles and standing in society, and dress codes set the tone of an organization. The reasons for these codes vary widely and change over time. In the 1960s, women generally could not wear pants at the office.[84] In the 1990s, many organizations went "corporate casual," but dress codes have begun to tighten up again, a trend fueled partly by an ongoing national debate about the decline of civility and partly by other forces.

Most often, however, dress codes are based on some notion of professionalism and functionality. In one medical school in Great Britain, the code states, "All students are expected to wear a clean and *smart* white coat whilst working in the clinical areas. All students should be *smartly presented* when visiting patients on the Wards or at General practices." Often these codes involve enforcement provisions that severely limit freedom of expression.

---

84 In January 1995, the California legislature finally "gave" women the right to wear pants at work.

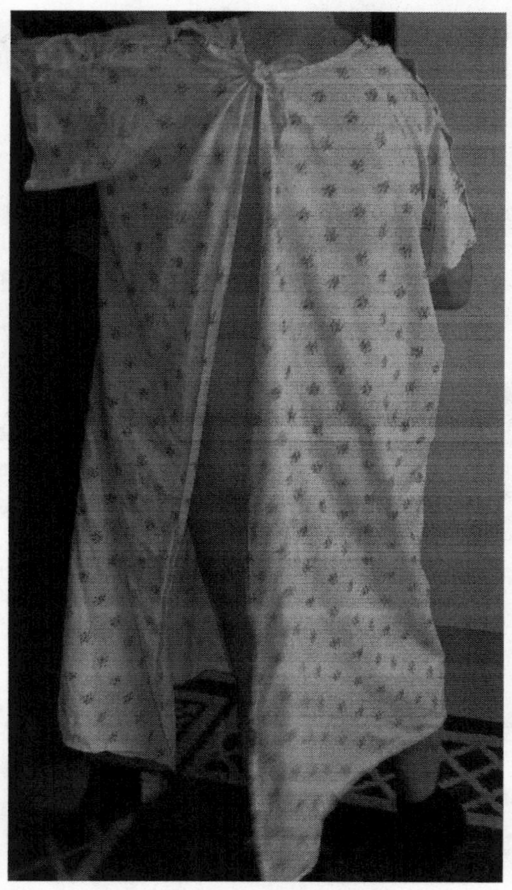

The seemingly innocuous concept of "functional attire" debases hospital patients, illustrating how the healthcare system tends to treat patients as plumbing systems in need of repair. One of the first ordeals faced by hospital patients is changing into a hospital gown; a drab, shapeless garment that is flimsy when seen from the front and completely humiliating when seen from behind. It is one of the more humbling fashion statements ever to be slid over the shoulders of an adult. It is far more denigrating even than prison uniforms. The gown is "functional" only from the point of view of medical personnel, who have easy access for exams and anesthesia.

Many doctors and nurses become oblivious to the dignity of the people with whom they are dealing, using language that denigrates patients, often in their presence. Says one doctor to another, looking at an image of a patient who is still in the scanner: "Livers like this don't last long." When the patient starts to cry, the doctor goes on to say: "I know how you feel."[85]

Stories of bedside abuse are legion. Many patients do not dare complain, scared to be "needled" in a painful way, or to be forgotten when beds are made. Worse still, physicians routinely ignore patient privacy, asking the most personal questions within earshot of others. This "pumping for information" shows no respect for patient sensitivities. The process is often so crude that other patients become uncomfortable.

At present, more is being done to address the concerns of patients, but old habits die slowly and bedside denigration is still very much alive. Some creative nurses have come up with new designs to replace the hospital gown. Their market strategy: promoting the *patient's dignity* by exposing less of their bodies.

The Costs of Denigration

Attention to dignity and the amelioration of denigration can help reduce costs, enhance efficiency, and promote a healthier work climate. In an ideal world, we would all pursue the goal of human dignity for its own sake. But real-world decision-makers face strong pressures to perform cost-benefit analyses before broaching any new initiatives. Common sense tells us that denigration can exact a tremendous psychological toll on individuals. At the organizational level, these costs are harder to quantify. But the costs are there.

For a number of reasons, calculating the costs of workplace denigration will never be an exact science. The symptoms of denigration—such as stress, burnout, violence, depression, fatigue, and so on—may have multiple causes, including illness, family problems, or social conditions. Furthermore, workplace denigration can be part of a larger cultural pattern, and it cannot be isolated from the broad spectrum of human activities. Finally, denigration is hard

---

[85] Terry Mizrahi, *Getting Rid of Patients: Contradictions in the socialization of physicians* (New Brunswick, NJ: Rutgers University Press, 1986).

to analyze mathematically. What is the long-term cost of distrust and miscommunication?

Some studies have been done to measure the economic effect of gender and race barriers in the labor market. However, these studies extend no further then the earnings ratio of female-to-male or black-to-white workers in equal positions, ignoring the broader costs to society of minimizing opportunities for women and minorities.

In some cases, the government has targeted extreme denigration for strictly humanitarian reasons. The worst abuses of child labor were outlawed in the United States on humanitarian grounds. But such cases are exceptions. Organizations are driven largely by economic imperatives, and the case for dignity as a wise business decision must be based on hard data. That data should demonstrate, for example, that denigration results in compensatory behaviors or coping mechanisms that cause:

- Increased stress and burn-out, illness, chronic disease, and absenteeism.
- Workplace rage directed at the victimizer or the organization as a whole.
- Disregard for deadlines, target quotas, or organizational goals.
- Anger directed at weaker persons in the workplace or the home.

Denigration causes decreased productivity and higher turnover, chronic illness, violence, and suicide—measurable phenomena with staggeringly high economic costs.

Litigation. The legal costs associated with unlawful denigrating actions, such as discrimination and disregard for OSHA or EPA regulations, are considerable. The Texaco case cited at the beginning of this chapter, with its $176 million settlement, is only one of many such class-action lawsuits. Countless similar suits lead to private settlements that are not reported by the press. The total organizational cost of anti-discrimination lawsuits goes beyond court verdicts and settlements to include liability insurance premiums and the time spent on such matters by in-house legal counsel. The price tag is in the billions, and every organization pays its share of the total.

Lost Productivity. Between 1994 and 1996, the cost of stress-related lost productivity exceeded $100 billion in the United States.[86] In 1998, the Trade Union Council of Great Britain estimated that workplace stress cost employers about $8 billion per year, excluding indirect costs such as lower morale and family stress. The Trade Union Council launched a major campaign to combat job insecurity, bullying, and forced overtime. In Britain, six million working days are lost to stress-related health problems every year.[87]

Violence. Approximately seven hundred workers are the victims of workplace homicide in the United States each year. Of these homicides, disgruntled employees or clients are responsible for about 15 percent. The cost of violence at work in America exceeds $55 million in lost wages alone. When lost productivity, legal expenses, property damage, diminished public image, increased security and other factors are included, total losses from workplace violence can be measured in the billions of dollars.[88]

A thirty-two-country study found that violent interactions at work include bullying, mobbing, and harassment, all forms of denigration.[89] Examples include behaviors such as criticizing people openly, isolating persons by leaving them without social contacts, or incessant ridiculing. In Sweden, an estimated 10 to 15 percent

---

86 Jerome Murray, "Coping with Stress," <http://www.betteryou.com/coping.htm> (accessed March 1, 2005).

87 The UK National Work-Stress Network, "The Costs of Work Related Stress," <http://www.workstress.net/costs.htm> (accessed March 4, 2005); Trade Union Council Website <http://www.tuc.org.uk/> (accessed March 4, 2005).

88 Eric F. Sygnatur and Guy A. Toscano, "Work-related Homicides: The Facts," In *Compensation and Working Conditions* (U.S. Department of Labor, Bureau of Labor Statistics, Census of Fatal Occupational Injuries, 2000); Occupational Safety & Health Administration (OSHA), "Workplace Violence Awareness and Prevention: Facts and Information," http://www.osha.gov/workplace_violence/wrkplaceViolence.PartI.html (accessed April 6, 2005).

89 Chappell and Di Martino, 1998.

of all suicides are related to this kind of denigrating behavior.[90] In Germany, the average annual cost of mobbing has been calculated at 200,000 DM in direct costs per one thousand workers, plus indirect costs of 100,000 DM per year.[91] The organizational costs of these behaviors are considerable.

Examples of violent behavior at work:

homicide	bullying	rape	mobbing
robbery	victimizing	wounding	intimidation
battering	threats	physical attacks	ostracism
kicking/biting	punching	spitting	offensive messages
scratching	shouting	abuse	squeezing and pinching
stalking	innuendo	swearing	harassment
name-calling	rude gestures	hostile behavior	deliberate silence
aggressive posturing	interfering with equipment		

(From Chappell and Di Martino, 1998.)

While it is impossible to put a precise price tag on denigration, the incidence of such closely associated problems as legal actions, productivity-sapping stress, and workplace violence indicates that the costs are very high indeed. Unlike the fixed operating costs associated with operating a business, denigrating behavior is a cost that most organizations are in a position to reduce, if not eliminate. Yet organizations continue to spend large amounts of money and energy to mitigate the symptoms of denigration, rather than trying to cure the disease. The morally correct and economically sensible solution is to make human dignity the rule in all workplace interactions.

###

90 Ibid.

91 Ibid.

Chapter Five

Searching for Dignity

The concept of dignifying has traditionally been suspect in the business and academic worlds. But a new trend is afoot in business schools and executive offices. As organizations become more dependent on highly skilled knowledge workers, management is learning that success depends in large part upon retaining these valuable employees. Furthermore, management is finally acknowledging that a relaxed worker with a balanced life is more productive in the long term. Enlightened companies have established flexible hours, daycare programs, telecommuting, and other programs designed to ease work-life tensions. Companies are beginning to consider employee loyalty—which is linked to dignity—as a competitive advantage. This chapter provides examples of company-strengthening dignifying behaviors on the personal, institutional, and group level.

Leadership

True leaders do more than direct; they inspire. Such leaders are richly rewarded in our society because they set a good example and motivate followers to broaden their horizons and strive for excellence.

> Before he retired, Charles was a true leader. As CEO of a high-tech firm, he was awarded a prestigious prize for his efforts to commercialize the scientific results of innovative research. Yet it was his keen understanding of the importance of the dignity and humanity of his workforce that distinguishes him from so many managers. Charles managed by walking around. He wanted to keep up with the highly specialized research performed by individual employees and to weave their individual contributions together into meaningful and profitable projects. The goal of his daily walk-throughs was to learn from others, not to exert control. This exercise put employees in the driver's seat and made Charles a facilitator, not an order-giver.

This technique was not unique to Charles. Three things made him a genuinely dignifying and successful business leader:

- He observed changes—such as new family pictures—in the workplace, and he showed an interest in them. Charles was also a keen observer of behavior. He often helped resolve issues outside the workplace. When a child was sick or a problem had occurred, he remembered to ask about it the next time he saw the employee.
- He did not hide his family life from employees. If he did not show up for a meeting, he always gave an honest reason, however personal, because he felt that others had a right to know.
- He visited with support staff as well as scientific personnel, and discussed substantive issues with them. He understood that these workers influenced the work climate. He considered them professionals in their fields who needed to learn and grow. For example, he encouraged cafeteria managers to go to conferences and trade shows and to report what they had learned.

Charles was a leader who believed that each worker has a right to a "covenantal relationship," a relationship that fulfills deep needs, deals constructively with conflict and change, and gives work meaning. Charles knew that such relationships entail vulnerability, because they acknowledge mutual dependence. He took that risk because he knew the rewards were plentiful and because his own sense of dignity was well established. His dignifying was fully reciprocated.[92]

---

92 Max DePree, *Leadership is an Art* (New York: Dell Publishing, 1989).

Roving Leadership

Roving leadership refers to the indispensable people at all levels who are there when others need them. Roving leadership is the mark of a participatory organizational culture in which workers play a part in decision-making and are willing to accept problem ownership.[93] Roving leadership acknowledges each worker's ability to take charge beyond the narrow terms laid out in a job description.

Roving leadership was missing at a suburban Chicago hospital in 1998. Claiming that hospital rules prohibited them from leaving the facility, medical personnel refused to attend to a critically wounded boy who lay on the walkway outside the emergency room. Medical professionals ignored their professional ethic in deference to petty bureaucratic rules, allowing the child to die.[94]

"Roving" is more than leadership of co-workers. It refers to the truck driver who stops to help a motorist in distress and the teacher who steps outside the curriculum to grasp a "teachable moment." Roving implies alertness and an ability to bend the rules for a good cause. It implies an organizational culture where the employee is treated as a motivated contributor with sound judgment. Whereas the control-focused manager may see roving as shirking, the dignifying manager sees it as an expression of the *discretion* exercised by any competent, intelligent, and trusted worker.

Worker access to the Internet raised concerns in many human resources departments that employees were abusing the privilege. Some managers reported abuses such as surfing pornographic Web sites, reading one another's e-mail, mass-mailing jokes, and even

---

93 Ibid.

94 Jeremy Manier and William Recktenwald, "Hospital changes policy after death of 15-year-old boy only steps from the emergency room," *Chicago Tribune*, May 18, 1998. Chicago police criticized this "outrageous behavior" by hospital workers. At one point, police said, they were rebuffed when they asked hospital staff for a stretcher or gurney to help carry the boy into the hospital. An officer ultimately had to commandeer a wheelchair after hospital staff members refused to leave the building or dispense equipment to help save the boy. "They simply ignored us. Their people are out there having a smoke while this kid is lying there. I have never seen anything like this."

starting up Web-based businesses on company servers. Alarmed, companies stepped up monitoring. Forty percent of companies now monitor phone conversations, 10 percent tape them, and 15 percent read employee e-mail.[95] Yet some companies view open Internet access at work as a necessary component of roving leadership. Some organizations condone private Internet-based activities by their staff members, recognizing the potential for cultivating entrepreneurial partnerships, creativity, and growth. This atmosphere of freedom and support can produce multiple joint ventures. These policies are based on the dignifying notion that an atmosphere of freedom and trust is beneficial for the organization as a whole. Strict control and spying are anathema to creativity, which is at the core of any successful organization.

Labor Laws

In April 1998, the prime minister of Finland became a father and took three weeks of paid parental leave. He was following the country's labor laws, which are binding for every Finn. Yet in only two countries, Finland and the United States, did the story merit front page newspaper coverage. Paternal leave, which acknowledges the importance of family responsibilities in the lives of *all* parents, is taken for granted in most European countries. Work and family, factory and

> In the summer of 1998, the United Auto Workers (UAW) locals in two General Motors plants went on strike. GM responded with a shutdown and most of its operations stood idle for several weeks. Weeks later, negotiators reached a final agreement. This agreement contained a clause that in each plant and on each work floor, GM would form committees to address everyday matters that, left unattended, could cloud the nationwide collective labor negotiations. After generations of hardball tactics on both sides, the agreement suggested a modicum of common sense. At the very least, the agreement indicated that labor and management both recognized that the insults and indignities of factory life must be addressed at the local level.

95 James Coates, "World Wide Wastrels: We Know You've Got Mail," *Chicago Tribune*, May 25, 1998.

neighborhood, office and home are thought of as complementary aspects of a well-balanced life.

Most labor laws are designed to create humane work conditions. Many companies simply work within the parameters of the law. Others, however, have a managerial climate that views labor laws as unnecessary impositions by a government bureaucracy, and they focus their effort on circumventing and reducing the impact of these laws.

Employee-centered companies see government regulations as the bare minimum, and focus not on avoiding sanctions, but on creating a healthy and productive work environment. These companies believe that high-quality products and services are the result of a high-quality work life that allows employees to reach their potential. Ben & Jerry's, the Waterbury, Vermont, ice cream maker, made these principles part of their mission statement, which states that the company is committed to maintaining "a deep respect for individuals inside and outside the Company and for the communities of which they are a part." Some companies, albeit few, have encouraged the formation of trade unions. Other organizations have created an environment where questions of labor law are essentially moot, because the organization goes well beyond minimal legal compliance.

> The founders of Illinois-based TUSC, a highly successful private consulting firm, attribute their success to a strong value system, clear-cut goals, and the hiring of people who share their values. Says an owner, "In everyday life, you do what is right, you don't do it because you can make money. TUSC isn't made up of people having to live with two faces. The faces they wear at work are the same faces they wear at home." This commitment to integrity, hard work, and responsibility guides the hiring practices of the company. Not all technicians, however skilled, are right for the company. "We need people who fit our culture in terms of sharing integrity or trust. They have to be long-term thinkers. If a client has a million-dollar budget and we can do the job for a dollar, we do it for a dollar. That mentality must be shared

> by everyone in the firm." One TUSC employee affirmed that claim: "In this world driven by greed, it is hard to find a company founded on old-fashioned values. We are lucky to have leaders who strive to be the best without crossing the moral line. Nobody has to worry about whether or not they are going to have a job tomorrow because they refused to do something today that they didn't feel was right."[96]

TUSC forms teams of employees that blend their work duties with family and community responsibilities. Employees are trusted collaborators, and the company treats them with respect. At the best organizations, personnel policies are driven by a desire to maximize human potential, not by fear of legal complaints.

Solidarity

Former Polish president Lech Walesa started his career as an electrician at the Gdansk shipyards during a period of growing labor unrest. He became an activist and was instrumental in creating and leading the Solidarnosc (Solidarity) trade union. The union gained the loyalty of the workers and became a potent anti-Communist force because it tackled a core problem of Polish society: the corrupting power of bureaucracy, which slowly drains the social dynamism of any movement, including the labor movement. In the Western world, Solidarnosc gained the support of everyone—the political left and right, trade unions and employer organizations, even the Pope, because Solidarnosc seemed to signify a rebirth of freedom and idealism. Artists were inspired by the call for more and real power to the workers, whose needs were all but ignored by the bureaucratic old guard. Movies were made and songs written. A mural in Paris read:

---

96 "Building Business by Doing the Right Thing: Trio Behind Lombard-Based TUSC Follows that Route," *Chicago Tribune*, February 22, 1998.

Liberté,
Egalité,
Fraternité...
Solidarité.

The mural was copied onto posters and t-shirts, as many people in France identified with the rebellion of the workers against a rigid, authoritarian state.

Worker solidarity is a major vehicle of what might be thought of as horizontal dignifying. It does not have to take the organizational form of a labor union or a professional association, although these organizations cannot exist without solidarity. The feeling of "being in this together" can be spontaneous and short-lived, or organic and enduring. Most solidarity movements are reactive in nature and come about when people feel that their worth, voice, and dignity are threatened. Two examples illustrate the force of solidarity as a dignifying process:

> In May of 1998, New York City implemented sanctions to regulate taxis and to correct the "uncivilized" behavior of some cabbies. The cab drivers, feeling insulted and ignored, organized a one-day strike. The strike was largely successful, mobilizing many cab drivers and bringing New York City to a halt. Journalists reporting on the case noted that most cab drivers were not unionized and would lose a day's much-needed income. The drivers, however, looked beyond the economic calculation. "I haven't lost anything," said a striking

cabbie when asked about his lost wages. "I've gained my self-respect."[97]

In early 1998, Caterpillar Inc. and the United Auto Workers settled a six-year labor conflict. Caterpillar survived the long strike by hiring replacement workers and placing many managers on the assembly line. The initial agreement included relatively few company concessions. Tired by the long battle, union members reluctantly accepted the settlement. During the ratification process, some members declared their opposition to the agreement because the company refused to grant amnesty to 160 fired union laborers. Paraphrasing one of the strikers' sentiments, "We had to stand up for real American values. We union members will accept Cat's request and not punish the scabs. But we will not accept any deal that keeps our brothers out of the plant. They are Cat's prisoners of war, and we will set them free." The initial agreement was rejected by a vote of 58 to 42 percent. After the vote, Caterpillar management, realizing that the cost of accepting the activists' demand was relatively small, gave in on this point, giving an enormous boost to worker solidarity and morale. The activists in the UAW brought to the rank-and-file a renewed sense of dignity. [98]

---

[97] Personal interview.

[98] Danny Booher and Frank Forrestal, "Caterpillar is Forced to Recall Fired Unionists—UAW members ratify contract in close vote," *The Militant* 62, no. 13 (1998): http://www.themilitant.com/1998/6213/6213_1.html ; "Cat Workers Fighting Example," *The Militant* 62, no. 13 (1998): http://www.themilitant.com/1998/6213/6213_6.html; <www.fortunecity.de/boerse/delta/183/slate/motley_fool/98-03-12/mo. This would have been legally and socially impossible in most European countries, where solidarity is stronger. In the mind of the European worker, strike-breaking is a grave indignity. Therefore, scabs and replacement workers have no right to respect and place themselves at great risk of public scorn and social abandonment. Just as the Amish "turn their backs" on outcasts, declaring them socially dead, so many a scab has been forced to move from the neighborhood.

Territorial Claims

When architects design workspaces, they like to focus on functionality and quality of life in the workplace. The point is to create a pleasant and hygienic environment in terms of both physical and mental health. In downtown business districts, suburban industrial parks, and in "brown-field" redevelopment plans, a fair amount of attention is paid to pleasing lines, eye-catching details, and attractive landscaping. On the plazas of lower Manhattan, lunching workers attend open-air musical and dance presentations. In the complex that houses the Chicago Mercantile Exchange, a shopping mall and terraces are part of the work environment. A major auto distribution facility in suburban Chicago has a broad green band around its miles-long perimeter.

Why all this investment in form? In a 1998 study, the real estate department at the Wharton School of the University of Pennsylvania reported that corporations were dedicating more space to communal uses and making work environments more functional and appealing.[99] According to the study, corporations provide, on average, 155 square feet of space per office worker. Enlightened senior managers base their decisions about space allocation on the idea that the office is where people live during working hours. According to the Wharton study, firms in a service-based economy must provide an office environment that attracts and retains value-added employees. (Another factor, of course, is that investment in commercial real estate is considered prudent capital management.)[100]

---

99 Steve Kerch, "By any measure, office is where you live during work," *Chicago Tribune*, February 26, 1998.

100 Given the end of the bubble economy of the late 1990s, a strong note of caution is in order. One wonders whether the trends cited here, which appear to attest to a new-found respect for the dignity of workers, will prove anything but a phase produced by the stunning demand for knowledge workers during the technology sector/Internet boom of the late 1990s. Stories in the business pages following the collapse of the stock market certainly attest to the collapse of any of the upstart firms that offered employees such office perks as weekly massage therapy in addition to generous stock options.

Space is empty until someone claims it. Everyone needs to stake out territory. This territorial instinct is manifested by symbols of recognition. We claim our homes not only with a deed or lease, but also by marking our walls and mantels with art, photos, and *objets d'art*. This marking fulfills an important psychological need. At work, we claim territory as well, because corporate space is both public and private. We find this phenomenon in the possessive behavior of workers regarding space and awareness of spatial "rights." Even assembly line workers mark their space by decorating their toolboxes with bumper stickers and other personal insignia.

We start this game of claiming as children by personalizing our bedrooms. As adults, we do the same with "our" desks and "our" offices. We have come a long way toward recognizing the individual's need for space since the old days of huge typing halls and long rows of standing desks. The modern manager knows that this need can be fulfilled without the loss of productivity. While *Dilbert* cartoons may joke about the "cubicle-ization" of America, cubicles do satisfy at least two psychological needs. On the one hand, they provide the open ceiling effect of what, in the sixties, were called "office gardens." On the other hand, they furnish a territory that can be claimed by the "owner" and acknowledged by others. They also give employees the responsibility for maintaining their own "nests."

Recognizing Opposition

Open-minded, dignifying CEOs establish a rapport with the workforce that makes it possible to express differences of opinion without being considered a danger to the company. Managers dignify employees when they create an organizational platform for diverse opinions. Good managers understand the value of "loyal opposition" and realize that mutual respect underlies any such relationship. Loyal opposition implies that staff and management have an investment in an organization's success. A climate that recognizes loyal opposition is valuable for workers, who are free to express their opinions, and for managers, who receive valuable input and can share responsibility. Wise managers understand that loyal opposition is normal and healthy, not threatening, and that silence does not always constitute agreement. Janis has promoted the concept of the "devil's advocate" or the "permanent opposition" figure as one method to fight the tendency toward groupthink.[101]

Large organizations, where communications technology has made non-work-related communication among employees natural and inevitable, should channel these communications so they contribute to the organization's success:

> One university has a newsletter called, appropriately enough, *University for Whom?* The publication tries to voice the opinions of workers, students, and patients in the university. The group behind this newspaper claims "the entire program [of the university] is being carried out in the most arbitrary manner and behind the backs of the people. We have called our newspaper *University for Whom?* precisely to bring to the fore the decisive need for the people to have their say on the fundamental aims and direction of the university."

Not only does this group claim a stake in the affairs of the university, they can do so with the full acknowledgment of the administration. Whether it survives long or not, the newsletter signals a dignifying climate. The same climate is apparent in the free flow of ideas in the university-based online chat room, "The Academy."[102]

Enlightened managers realize that platforms for discussing opinions are a good thing. They also know that without these platforms, gossip will flourish, growing like weeds that strangle the productive life of an institution.

---

101 Janis, 1982. According to Janis, the opposition figure can be valuable only if the person playing this role is safe from managerial contempt and punishment.

102 University of Illinois at Chicago. The chat room operates largely unfettered, although the university does monitor chat room discourse.

Customer Satisfaction

Chapter Four looked at the denigration, under the guise of functionality, of clients and patients of healthcare organizations. Thankfully, new views of customers, patients, and clients are taking root. Under the influence of the various social movements of the last forty years, the managerial view of clients and patients is changing dramatically. As Robert Fisher observed: "The numerous human rights movements indicate that we are beginning to value people more highly than we have in the past. As these movements gain momentum, *people as people* will move higher on the priority list, while the personal accumulation of wealth and power will decline."[103]

Customer satisfaction has become a goal (or at least a slogan) for many companies, not only for those companies that cater to a wealthy clientele. Long ago, Henry Ford claimed, "Of course clients have a choice of color, as long as it is black." Most car designs today are based on customer surveys and focus groups. Unfortunately, the goal of customer satisfaction is usually skin-deep and market-driven, and does not reflect a new respect for the customer. Still, these attitudes are potentially dignifying for employees. As Kanter makes clear, "Service industries depend on their employees to give them a competitive advantage. Only corporations that pay attention to their workforce will move ahead."[104]

A similar change is apparent in the healthcare industry. Doctors and other medical professionals pay more attention to patients' and families' opinions. Patient choice has become a force that professionals recognize. Nursing and medical schools have resurrected the notion of proper bedside manner, sometimes in innovative ways, as the following example shows.

> To help break old views and habits, students at the University of Chicago's Pritzker School of Medicine performed a play.

---

[103] Robert W. Fisher, "The future of energy," *The Futurist* 31, p. 43, September-October 1997.

[104] Rosabeth Moss Kanter, *Rosabeth Moss Kanter on the Frontiers of Management* (Boston: Harvard Business School Press, 1997).

> A professor organized a production of "This Is a Test: One Girl's Fight with Cancer," written by eighth-grader Shenita Peterson. The play was intended to illustrate what it means to be a patient and to remind medical students that patients are more than disease states. The play addresses Shenita's feeling that she was treated like a "non-person" by some doctors, who would talk among themselves as if she wasn't there. She also felt put down by dubious remarks from doctors, such as "I know what you're feeling."[105]

The more holistic approach to patient needs suggests progress toward greater dignity in all healthcare relationships.

Empowerment

The vast literature on empowerment suggests that empowerment and dignifying are not the same: one is a means; the other is an end. Applying the means without a commitment to the end is futile. However, when empowerment is a core goal of the organization, dignity is more likely to be valued by managers. When workers actually own a company, the empowerment concept is apt to be more broadly implemented. Home Depot works from that premise, as does United Airlines (the airline's economic and legal woes notwithstanding). The following letter, written to United Airlines by a passenger, underscores how that company allows employees to protect their own dignity in potentially denigrating situations.

> An award should go to the United Airlines gate agent in Denver for being smart and funny—and for making her point—when confronted with a passenger who deserved to fly as cargo. During the day, at Denver Airport, a crowded United flight was canceled. A single agent was re-booking a long line of inconvenienced travelers. Suddenly, an angry passenger pushed his way to the desk. He slapped his ticket

[105] Personal observation.

down on the counter and said loudly, "I *have* to be on this flight and it has to be *first class*."

The agent replied, "I'm sorry sir. I'll be happy to try to help you, but I've got to help these folks first and I'm sure we'll be able to work something out." The passenger was unimpressed. He asked loudly, so that the passengers behind him could hear, "Do you have any idea who I am?"

Without hesitating, the gate agent smiled and grabbed the public address microphone. "May I have your attention please?" she began, her voice bellowing throughout the terminal. "We have a passenger here at the gate *who does not know who he is*. If anyone can help him find his identity, please come to Gate 17."[106]

Empowerment, as depicted in the writings of Brazilian educational theorist Paolo Freire, is sometimes built around the principle of human dignity. All too often, however, it is applied—and perceived—as simply another cost-cutting measure whereby employees gain greater managerial responsibility without the corresponding rewards.

For investors on Wall Street, corporations are a series of numbers, reflecting the balance-sheet reality of financial decisions. Many corporate headquarters, acting as absentee landlords, use the same approach when evaluating the performances of their subsidiary companies scattered around the globe. Businesses are moved, closed, or re-structured on orders from people who are largely detached from the social realities of the enterprise. Headquarters are less likely to witness the effects of NAFTA as American manufacturing jobs move across the border, but they do hear the cheers of stockholders. At the core of capitalist decision-making are abstract financial considerations and a worldview that holds that the rights of private ownership take precedence over those of other stakeholders.

---

[106] Source unknown.

Occasionally, workers are empowered to take control of the organizations they run.

In 1997, New York–based Leeds Manufacturing Co. closed its fabric cutting and sewing plant in Dawson, Georgia, after defaulting on a $770,000 loan. The plant's two hundred workers lost their jobs. The former plant manager and the local mayor arrived at a plan to reopen the plant as a cooperative, in which each worker would be an owner with a say in running the plant.

The mayor and manager vaulted the next two hurdles when the Southwest Georgia Rural Development Board offered an emergency loan of $150,000 and the foreclosing bank agreed to keep the plant off the auction block. The bank leased the property to the mostly women- and minority-owned cooperative, with no money down and rent payable at the end of the year. To make this offer, both the bank and the Development Board made exceptions to their normal way of operating. At the new worker-owned plant, the workforce is inspired, finding strength in the shared sacrifices. According to one worker, "The workers bring their own soap, paper towels, and toilet paper. They take turns cleaning the bathrooms. They use brooms and mops from home for the plant floor, mow the grass, pick up litter on their own time, and stop by to check on the plant after hours. . . . Employees work together in an adventure in efficiency and sacrifice while apparel plants continue to disappear across the South. I'm very proud to work here." Workers walk faster, take shorter lunch hours, and don't close their machines until the workday is over. But the changes go deeper in terms of performance, dedication, and spirit. "We're going to do whatever is necessary to make it work," says D. W. "We make our own decisions. It's no longer, 'The company says do this, do that.' It shows what can be done if we don't just lay down and roll over." The economics of the effort are also striking. An incentive pay system lets workers earn nearly double their old hourly pay

> if they meet productivity targets based on strict efficiency standards.[107]

The Dawson Workers-Owned Cooperative, LLC, became a reality because bureaucrats were willing to operate outside their normal way of doing business. An entire town changed course, as local textile workers became owners and teammates, dignifying each other in the process.

Celebrating Diversity

The post–Cold War global economy, a product of Western (particularly American) hegemony in world affairs, puts a premium on "diversity." The term implies not just demographic diversity, but a philosophical commitment to understanding and valuing the cultural differences that demographic changes have wrought. As we become more successful, we need to pay more attention to those to whom we paid no heed two generations ago. Minorities, women, and immigrants are recognized as legitimate players in the task of changing the corporate world and its culture. When diversity is celebrated, employees are valued for their uniqueness, rather than their interchangeability. Diversity encourages managers to view workers as human beings within a cultural context, not merely as extensions of machines.

We are standing at the threshold of a new era of corporate diversity. Managing diversity has become a specialty with its own tactics and vocabulary. The underlying message, however, is simple and significant: Those who embrace diversity enrich their work and their social lives, increase their potential, and become more capable of cooperation and teamwork. As the workforce becomes more diverse, human dignity takes center stage. Each group must deal with the viewpoints and sensitivities of others, and managers strive to be seen as fair and unbiased.

Owing to its colonial history, the tiny South American nation of Suriname is a heterogeneous society with no majority ethnic group.

---

107 Catherine Merlo, "The triumph of Dawson's textile workers," *Rural Cooperatives* 65, p. 12-16, March/April 1998.

Suriname's ethnic diversity has its roots in Dutch colonization and the importation of African slaves and indentured laborers from India and Indonesia. Various ethnic groups flock to certain jobs and trades based on historical patterns and family tradition. At the country's telephone company, the bookkeeping department consists predominantly of Asian Indians, while cable installers are mostly Creole and transmission services are mainly in the hands of ethnic Chinese. This clustering places the coordinating managers in a position of constant balancing. Most workers recognize the need to maintain balance and fairness, and the trade union has members from all ethnic groups. The need for harmony leads to an awareness of the unique place of other workers as individuals as well as group members. That awareness is central to the dignifying process. The complex forces at work in a multi-ethnic environment are not necessarily distracting or destructive; if channeled correctly, they can enrich the workplace.[108]

Too much ethnic awareness can lead to nepotism. In Ghana, for example, where soccer is about as popular as basketball, football, and baseball put together in the United States, many soccer matches are arranged between villages or towns with different tribal and family backgrounds. This generally works out well. However, when blood relations override functional roles, players on a team tend to pass the ball only to members of their clan. This is called *kokofuball*, a symbol of dysfunctional ethnocentrism. Celebrating diversity means not engaging in kokofuball.[109]

Too often, personnel policies have been shaped by a kokofuball ethic, resulting in managerial incompetence, employee resentment, and organizational ineffectiveness as members of the dominant family, group, or class are promoted beyond their ability and others are excluded from consideration. For many years, becoming a longshoreman in Baltimore's Dundalk Harbor or New York's Red Hook Terminal virtually required a job applicant to be related to a current employee.

---

108 Personal observation.

109 Ibid.

Quite a few companies have policies in place to battle kokofuball tendencies, while at the same time celebrating diversity.

###

Chapter Six

Promoting Dignity: Concrete Approaches

While it is easy to identify with the moral issues raised in the earlier chapters, identification and awareness are insufficient to produce change. Promoting dignity requires first reflection, then taking a stand, and finally taking action. This chapter offers suggestions for encouraging attitudinal change in the individual manager or worker.

> "What is correct and virtuous is defined in terms of universalizable standards, reflectively constructed by the individual, of justice, natural rights, and humanistic respect for all persons, regardless of sex, age, ethnicity, race, or religion. . . . Post-conventional thinkers recognize that among the terms of any voluntary and rationally based contract to form a society, justice, fairness, and natural rights must reign."
>
> (Shweder, et. al., 1992)

We label our suggestions under two headings: the prevention of denigration and the promotion of dignity. This is somewhat artificial, since dignifying should be thought of as a continuum, ranging from all-out denigration to full-fledged adherence to the principal of dignity. However, some managerial actions can be classified as dignifying while many others serve only to prevent denigration. We will use this distinction to the extent that it is useful as we suggest steps for improvement.

Advocating prescriptive techniques to help dignify others may be perceived as moralizing. In a broad sense, it certainly is. Dignifying others is based on a well-developed sense of morality and the ability to make moral judgments. Incorporating the dignity of others into one's judgment indicates a high level of moral development—what Kohlberg refers to as the "post-conventional level" of moral development.[110] The eminent Swiss psychologist Jean Piaget called this the construction of *moral autonomy*.[111]

---

[110] James Weber, "Managers' Moral Reasoning: Assessing their responses to three moral dilemmas," *Human Relations* 43, no. 7 (1990): 687-702.

[111] Iordanis Kavathatzopoulos, "Kohlberg and Piaget: Differences and similarities," *Journal of Moral Education* 20, no.1 (1991): 47-54.

Previous chapters have argued that dignified interactions reduce stress and social distance in tough decision-making situations.[112] However, dignity must be defended and encouraged not only in moral terms. It must be argued in practical terms that make a compelling case to managers who face pressures from executives, corporate board members, and their own profit motivations to focus on the bottom line. Dignifying workers, colleagues, customers, and ourselves must become a *reasonable* goal. There are many obstacles, including the fear of being perceived as a "wimp" within the highly masculine and intensely competitive culture of many organizations. Managers confront the pressing question of how to reconcile proposed behavior and attitude changes with pre-existing beliefs and expectations. That is, dignifying as an attitude change still needs to fit a person's *sense of coherence*—a sense that Aaron Antonovsky describes as the dynamic feeling of confidence that comes from the comprehensibility, manageability, and meaningfulness of the world in which we work and live.[113] Not only must we be able to understand ourselves, others in our environment need to understand our actions as well. Unexpected behavioral changes may make people disoriented, resulting in skepticism and avoidance.

Workers and managers benefit from combining work and private life (albeit in a bounded manner) and from treating outward emotional expressions as socially acceptable. A 1997 study led by Joanne Martin highlighted a trend toward "boundary crossing," an alternative to traditional bureaucratic behavior. Martin and her colleagues described an ideal organizational climate in which dignifying is the centerpiece of human interaction among peers.

Choosing the High Road

There are two paths to organizational power and status: the high road, which involves forging ahead, outpacing others, and using one's talents to outshine others; and the common road, based on keeping

112 Folger and Skarlicki, 1998.

113 Aaron Antonovsky, *Health, Stress, and Coping* (San Francisco: Jossey-Bass Publishers, 1979).

others down and preventing them from using their opportunities and talents. For several reasons, the common road is the one most often traveled. Most people believe that their own talent, opportunity, and potential is limited, and they choose not to empower others, who are generally seen as rivals. Also, work and society as a whole are organized around a bureaucratic, hierarchical control structure. Delegating authority (i.e., power) becomes a "salami-slicing" exercise, with managers manifesting their power by withholding "slices." Finally, competing on the high road requires a high level of self-confidence, security, and moral development, as well as a well-developed ability to trust others.

Trusting others implies a willingness to take risks.[114] When trust and confidence are low (often because of an inability to take risks) and unpredictability is high, managers and others in authority usually fall back on controlling by withholding. Only those with considerable self-confidence can reach the high road. What is more, organizational reward systems often recognize the extremes of behavior, but fail to encourage the average person to take the high road. Many organizations use their annual dinners to recognize those who go "beyond the call of duty," implying that their dignifying actions are outside the norm. Meanwhile, we publicize and punish genuinely abhorrent behavior, such as deliberately putting employees in harm's way by locking the fire escapes. By focusing on the extreme and sensational, we forgo practical lessons regarding dignity and denigration in our daily lives. When we focus only on the few winners, ignoring the accomplishments of many others, we voluntarily diminish our experiences.

When we use legal limits to define denigrating actions, in the belief that an action is acceptable as long as it isn't criminal, we show that we understand neither the role of the legal system nor our responsibilities as human beings. The law defines but a small part of a broad system of norms that define our society. Relying only on the legal system and the annual award dinner belittles our roles as citizens, workers, parents, and neighbors. In practical terms, we have to commit ourselves to certain ideas: that we should compete

---

[114] Seligman, 1997.

with a sense of sportsmanship, that we can gain power and influence without keeping those below us down, and that by uplifting others, we are uplifted.

Managers whose worldview consists of a single-minded drive for bigger profits and more efficient operations see no need for a discourse on dignity, because they believe that if something cannot be expressed in dollars, it isn't worth pursuing. Thus, in those organizations where the bottom line has become the only line, dignifying can only be justified by its impact on the profit margin or its cost-cutting potential. This leads us to the paradox inherent in dignifying: it is not a means to an end, and cannot occur where it is pursued only for economic reasons. Dignifying for profit is not dignifying at all.

The organizational world is a *social* reality that may be driven by economic rationality, but is also deeply affected by other aspects of the human experience. Everyone in the organization brings emotions, values, needs, and fears to their daily work—feelings not dictated by economic logic. Most are capable of some degree of empathy, and few get pleasure from the pain of others. Difficult decisions that may involve pain for others should never be made automatically; managers must take into account the reality and consequences of human suffering. Good managers engage in soul-searching; they do not dehumanize themselves. Even when the bottom line is the most important consideration, it can never be the only consideration.

Ameliorating denigration and promoting dignity may require an attitude change, individually and collectively, that can be gauged by changes in organizational climate and the behavior of workers. One of the most important tasks of a dignifying manager is to foster clear two-way communication. In our modern service economy, the isolated, machine-bound worker who produces without significant human interaction is becoming rarer. By emphasizing two-way communication, managers help diminish alienation and demonstrate that the workplace is a truly human environment.

Embracing Democratic Dignity

It is possible to develop a worldview that emphasizes cooperation over competition, community needs over egotistical excess, negotiation over confrontation, and long-term quality of life over short-term profit. By declaring the need to embrace the dignity of each human being, we place ourselves squarely in the camp of those managerial theorists who work from a holistic human perspective. Even within the critical theories that view conflict as inherent in organizations, there are openings for dignity. Dignity is not a *tool* of conflict management or conflict reduction; it defines the arena in which constructive conflict occurs.

The first stage in the dignifying process is to incorporate these premises about human dignity, equality, and participation into the more mundane aspects of our lives on three levels:

- At the individual level, we need to change our attitudes through rigorous self-reflection.
- At the organizational level, we need behavioral change through long-term managerial focus on organizational climate and work processes.
- At the community level, we need to assess the place of the organization within the community.

Recognizing the dignity of each person means eliminating managerial cynicism, renouncing the tools of fear and manipulation, and rejecting the notion that human beings are inherently lazy, shirking, and untrustworthy. Embracing the goal of dignity is a process that depends on, and can feed, the moral development of the manager.[115] That is, accepting such a concept implies that the manager is willing and able to base his or her moral reasoning on chosen principles. The reciprocal nature of dignifying creates outward-spreading waves of moral, spiritual, and rational development throughout the organization.

Dignifying at the Individual Level

Awareness of dignity and denigration is only the first step toward changing one's work attitudes and behavior. Several additional steps

115 James Weber, 1990.

are addressed here.[116] These steps are all based on the notion that we need to keep reminding ourselves that we gain dignity by granting dignity. The suggestions included here focus on changing the *way* we do things.

The Contemplation Phase

During the contemplation phase, which can last from hours to months, managers must address several questions: How do we react to the ideas and arguments presented in this book? Is "organizational dignity" an oxymoron or do morality and decency require us to reflect on the dignity of the human beings we work with? We must scrutinize our motives and our beliefs about human beings, and face the fact that while dignity is often praised in the abstract, it is generally in short supply.

Made aware of how dignity can contribute to the quality of everyday work life, we must decide where we as individuals stand and what we can do. Managers must determine whether they have enough stake in their organizations to try to make a difference, and whether they have the insight to evaluate their own behavior honestly.

We can never read our own behavior, intentions, and actions without some bias. To examine our positions vis-à-vis others, we need a clear concept of what we are trying to accomplish, what hurdles may stand in our way and what the likely consequences are. In this phase, we must wrestle with such personal questions as whether the effort is worth the energy, how such an effort will be perceived, and who can be expected to support the initiative. And once these issues have been resolved, three additional questions must be addressed:

- Should I move forward with a plan to work on my own attitudes regarding dignifying?

---

[116] Prochaska and Diclemente have developed a theory of planned behavior change that includes the phases of pre-contemplation, contemplation, planning, implementation, execution, and maintenance. We refer to their theoretical model.

- Should I actively address the issue of dignifying in my own work environment?
- If the answer to both of these questions is yes, what should be the scope and manner of implementation? Should I attempt to prevent denigration, promote dignifying, or address both?

The Planning Phase

One should not undertake behavioral and attitude changes as though they were a new diet or exercise fad. It is best to begin slowly. Deliberate, thoughtful progress is more important than flamboyant enthusiasm.

Begin by assessing the denigrating and dignifying experiences you have witnessed, and the strategically chosen behavioral changes that could enhance dignity. Select two or three confidants and discuss these plans with them. In discussion, begin the process of articulating standards of behavior that demonstrate dignifying as well as examples of denigration. Standards that come to mind are:

- *Name memory.* Do I know and use the names of the people with whom I regularly interact at work? Am I on a first-name basis with receptionists as well as bosses?
- *Seeing the whole person.* What do I know about the life situations of the people I interact with, and how do I appreciate and express that knowledge? Do I know the names of their spouses and children? What do I know of their interests and hobbies?
- *Examining my own behavior.* How do I interact with the boss, peers, and subordinates in different situations? Are there differences based on rank, age, gender, ethnicity? How do I deal with interruptions?
- *Considering motivation.* What motivational strategies do I usually apply and how do I apply them? Do I use intimidation or manipulation to increase productivity?

- *Considering corrections.* When and how do I apply sanctions to others and myself?

If you don't know anything about the people in your work circle, there is probably a problem. If you know more about some than others, try to find out why. Are you wittingly or unwittingly encouraging staff to curry favor or to rat on others? Are you playing favorites? Or, do you try to stimulate open communication whenever the circumstances allow? How do you read yourself in these circumstances? Include steps for improvement in your plan of action, even if you think that you are doing a much better job of dignifying than others in your organization.

Communication style is a core part of dignifying behavior. Are you always understood? How do you assess that? Have you ever tried to communicate your instructions in a different way? When do you use e-mail, and when do you schedule face-to-face meetings? How good are you at listening? Do you probe for meaning? How do you solicit feedback?

> A sound managerial principle that works well for dignifying: *PRAISE IN PUBLIC, PUNISH IN PRIVATE.*

Motivational strategies such as strict supervision and carrot and stick are, at heart, denigrating. Genuine motivation is based on neither the carrot nor the stick, but on clear communication of mutual goals and respect for dignity. Discussion of tasks in advance, clear formulation of expectations, and frequent feedback demonstrate respect for staff members. Compliments on progress and results often have greater motivational value than wage increases and bonuses.

How do you behave when correcting mistakes or intervening in personnel conflicts? Respectful punishment in private, as well as principled interventions in public, are almost always understood as "high road" behavior. Corrective actions that take place in the context of a dialogue and can be constructed as learning moments are high-level dignifying behaviors. Hollering and wagging a big stick are denigrating everywhere, every time.

These are issues that you can address when setting up a plan to analyze and change behavior in your organization. An effective plan includes a dignifying manager profile that incorporates both a self-assessment and an evaluation of the work environment. The plan should be organized as a sequence of steps.

The main results of this planning stage should be:

- Identifying the goals by deciding what behavior should be modified within a set time period.
- Documenting progress by maintaining some form of self-documentation, such as a diary, to record experiences, comments, and reflections.
- Critiquing and revising the plan with trusted colleagues.

The Implementation Phase

When you are ready to implement your plan, start small and consider the possible reactions to your actions. Start a formal feedback process with some of your employees to address the issues in your plan. What do they think about your expectations? What problems have they had with your management and communication style? Do you give them room to maneuver, or do you micromanage? Ask how they have fared in doing their jobs, and whether you have been a help or a hindrance. If this seems daunting, you may want to start your dignifying experiment at home, with your spouse or children. The implementation phase is situation-specific and many aspects must be addressed in an incremental manner. Over time, proceed with more phases of your action plan's dignifying manager profile, and evaluate the problems that occur.

Execution

In the execution phase, it is no longer necessary to evaluate every nuance of your behavior, because you have internalized a dignifying attitude. At this point, you can begin to address dignity as a collective issue, worthy of the attention of everyone in the organization. The next chapter discusses achieving dignity within this larger context.

###

Chapter Seven

Dignifying Strategies in the Organization and the Community

At 4:30 each Friday afternoon, students and faculty of the Johns Hopkins School of Public Health and Hygiene (JHSPHH) enjoy happy hour with a glass of wine or beer and some chips. Participants play the piano or chess; people mingle and make plans for the weekend. Sometimes the dean shows up. But his presence is not important; his active support for these impromptu happenings is. He promotes situations where people can interact with peers, subordinates, and superiors in an atmosphere of collegiality, where the human side of every participant can emerge.

Johns Hopkins' Dean Henderson learned much from his experience in the diplomatic milieu of the World Health Organization. More than half of the JHSPHH student body and many of its faculty hail from abroad, making the school's International Festival of Food, Dance, and Clothing a memorable annual occasion, where students and faculty highlight their ethnic identities and their fundamental respect for one another.

Many organizations host similar events. Lucent Technologies, Inc. celebrates diversity by sponsoring an international food festival and language clubs, as well as other programs. Some units of larger organizations organize their own social rituals. One section of the Illinois Department of Public Health schedules a British-style high tea each Friday afternoon following its weekly staff meeting. The section chief (a native of the South Side of Chicago) arranges the tea as a way to allow personnel to socialize in a dignified setting. A business newsletter publisher holds poetry discussions on Friday afternoons after working hours to allow editors and other staff to keep their critical and intellectual faculties sharp.

Managers have many ways to create a work climate in which workers can step outside of their formal roles and show more of their personality and culture. Unfortunately, workplace activities intended to celebrate diversity or social cohesion are not always executed in a dignifying way. For dignity to thrive, there must be an explicit desire on the part of management for workers to feel comfortable in, and appreciate, each other's presence. Highlighting *each person's worth* within the organization is the key.

There are two ways for a manager to address dignity in the workplace. The first, ameliorating denigrating conditions, involves tackling critical workplace problems—problems that threaten the continued employment of the individual manager, and possibly even the viability of the organization. The other is to promote dignifying in a relatively healthy organization.

If a manager wishes to focus attention on dignity at work, what are the initial steps? First, a manager must assess the work setting and his or her potential to bring about positive change.[117] This evaluative activity can be organized around the formula of **S**(trengths), **W**(eaknesses), **O**(pportunities), **T**(hreats)[118], centering on such topics as:

- hierarchy
- leadership styles
- centralized/decentralized management
- civility and respect
- tolerance for emotion
- communication styles
- attitudes towards change
- trust/distrust
- formality and narrowness of job descriptions
- gender ratio
- control systems
- internal competition/cooperation

---

117 Harold Koontz, Cyril O'Donnell, and Heinz Weihrich, *Essentials of Management* (New York: McGraw-Hill, 1982).

118 Ibid.

- work/personal life separation
- intra-organizational networks

No two managerial projects designed to reduce denigration or to promote dignity can or should be the same. Successful implementation of dignity projects—whether incremental or sweeping, scattered or broad, freestanding or integrated—depends upon how well one has assessed the organizational context, which includes the perspectives of affected workers. A context analysis should include the issues outlined in the following sections.

Cynicism

In today's society, cynicism is everywhere, aimed at politics and politicians, religious and secular institutions, educational systems, the caring professions, and, especially, the work world. Organizational cynicism is a negative attitude toward one's employing organization. It has two dimensions: the conviction that the organization lacks integrity, and disparaging and critical behaviors consistent with these beliefs that negatively affect the organization. Can we care about dignity in such a negative environment? We cannot afford not to. Cynicism is a festering problem that can interfere with any effort to promote positive change. A sustained focus on dignity can help us break through the cycle of cynicism and negate its root causes. By reducing cynicism, a successful dignifying program can lead to competitive advantages in hiring, quality, productivity, and morale. An organization will likely have little trouble finding qualified workers, when the firm's own workforce takes on the role of volunteer "head hunters." When employees are proud to be part of the company, they voluntarily take responsibility for finding good job candidates. Being part of the decision-making process and having their opinions count is reward enough.

In today's global marketplace, cynicism is more intense than ever. Cynics see efforts aimed at quality improvement or organizational change as futile and stick to their "learned belief that fixable problems at work will not be resolved due to factors beyond the individual's control."[119] Many employees are modern-day

Diogenes, exuding philosophical contempt for their employers and society at large. Organizational cynicism is a defense mechanism, protecting people from disappointment and hurt in hopeless work environments. Cynicism is negative emotional energy that could be transformed into a force for dignifying. Organizations can overcome cynicism by acknowledging the *affective* or emotional aspects of cynicism, such as disgust, anger, distress, and shame, and by addressing the sources of that cynicism, such as the notion that integrity, fairness, honesty, and sincerity are ruses, and that there is a hidden agenda behind many managerial decisions. We can start by paying attention to signs of cynicism—smirks and sneers, rolling eyes, sarcastic humor—and attempt to understand its sources. Two examples illustrate this point:

> The U.S. Postal Service has an image problem. For evidence, one need look no further than the popular jokes about workplace shootings by disgruntled postal workers. (Widespread use of the expression "going postal" to describe an angry or violent outburst is but one example.) Having spoken with several managers in the USPS, my collaborator provides the following description of a dignifying approach to resolving this issue. One postmaster asked for volunteers from his staff to join a new task force charged with developing a plan to counter the image problem and the underlying problem of anger and cynicism within the organization. He authorized the task force to recruit members from the general public and the local Chamber of Commerce. The task force could meet in private or in public; he would not attend the meetings. The postmaster then made some very public, dramatic gestures. He had his office door removed and invited each of his employees for a "casual chat," during which he inquired about their families, their work satisfaction, and a host of other issues. With employees' knowledge and consent, he recorded these chats and analyzed the responses. All employees received a

[119] James W. Dean, Jr., Pamela Brandes, and Ravi Dharwadkar, "Organizational Cynicism," *Academy of Management Review* 23, no. 2 (1998): 341-352.

copy of the results, along with a request for comments and suggestions for improving the work climate. He also asked workers for slogans to post in the post office.

The task force started its work immediately, and some of its suggestions were implemented as soon as they reached the postmaster's desk. While the office's hours did not change, the doors were opened ten minutes ahead of the official opening time and stayed open a few minutes after closing time, a change that improved relations between postal workers and customers. Another suggestion of the task force was to introduce "360-degree evaluations," in which supervisors and workers evaluated each other and offered constructive advice. Customer complaints were treated as opportunities for improvement.

The project, now in its second year, has increased morale and reduced absenteeism. The postmaster understood that dignifying was the high road to long-term organizational betterment. The project's success has caught the attention of the office of the Postmaster General.[120]

Personal observations from one of my collaborators describe how this dignifying was the mainstay of a policy change in the Dutch police force, which was facing a similar image problem in the early 1970s, following a spate of bad publicity. Charges of racist tactics, and brutality following a demonstration in 1968, led to arrests of police officers on charges of corruption. At the national level and in some Dutch cities, social scientists were hired to help reduce bad public perceptions about the police. Moreover, cynicism was growing within the police force itself.

Police leadership responded by envisioning a more democratic police force in which police officers would be

---

[120] Personal interviews.

viewed first as fathers, sons, daughters, neighbors, friends, etc., and second as police officers. These humane professionals would wear uniforms for purposes of public recognition, not to signify hierarchy and separation. Police officers received training in how to be friendly, to answer questions and to refer residents and visitors to sights and public services. New training efforts focused on debunking stereotypes and eliminating racial profiling. Community policing, already widely accepted in the Netherlands, grew in popularity. Nightsticks were no longer standard issue and were replaced by foreign-language dictionaries and city address books. Crime prevention became as important as investigative and prosecutorial activities, and social control roles were reduced. For example, a new policy of flexible restraint encouraged officers to be neither too strict nor too adamant, emphasizing the officer's discretion and tact over rigid, bureaucratic rules.

To deal with crisis situations, special armed units, called "mobile brigades," were created. In these brigades, the men and women wear distinctive gear, get special training in crowd control and anti-terrorism, and have a different command structure. The existence of these rarely seen special forces means that the regular Dutch police force is not burdened with unpopular paramilitary duties. [121]

Other dignifying actions followed:

- A decades-long advertising campaign put the human face of the police officer everywhere, creating a positive image of the officer as a friendly helper.
- Children's shows were created for television and radio in which police officers helped people solve problems ranging from lost keys to flat tires. The name *Bromsnor* (meaning *cranky moustache* as well

[121] Personal observation.

as *moped*), taken from one such TV character, is now the nickname of many a police officer.

- The police adopted new uniforms, with less stark colors, fewer insignia, a closer resemblance to civilian clothing, and, most importantly, less battle gear.

There was another element in the humanizing effort of the Dutch police: Dutch television broadcasts many Hollywood police programs, where the emphasis is more on car chases than the human side of the fight against crime. Dutch screenwriters and novelists wrote police shows and books that de-emphasized violence and focused on the human factor. As in some American police programs, many of the characters in these programs blend family and work roles, but without the Hollywood framework of murder and mayhem.

The Dutch police task force used a holistic approach. The group realized that the human face of the police officer was the key to softening the blue line and enhancing the dignity of police and civilians alike.

Bromsnor vindt 64 jaar
oude fiets weer terug

Bromsnor finds a stolen sixty-four-year-old bicycle.

Cynicism is both a personal attitude and a reflection or symptom of a negative cultural climate. Widespread cynicism can lead to reduced productivity, poor morale, and a low-quality work life. Cynicism, however, is also indicative of a defensive reaction by people who are afraid to trust others and do not want to risk pain, denigration, and loss of face. By countering the causes of cynicism, this defensive energy can be redirected in a positive way to stimulate the process of dignifying.

Civility

Dignifying and denigration are expressed through interaction. A change in the quality or intensity of an interaction pattern can indicate a descent into denigration or the reverse. For example, confronted with the downsizing mantra of the last decade, many managers experienced a social distancing from the potential victims of these layoffs and chose not to maintain close social contacts with employees. The movement toward dignifying in an organizational environment is easily translated into a vision of civil discourse. Denigration, in fact, is often associated with uncivil or rude behavior—but it is important to remember that civility is by no means the same as dignity.

Civility is a social code reflecting the type of interaction that makes the majority of participants feel comfortable. (See also Bourdieu on taste and habitus.) Concepts of civility vary between generations and between subcultures: the only universal is the concept of civility itself. When we speak of the general code of civility in the United States, we are typically referring to a middle-class code of interaction with roots in white Anglo-Saxon Protestant conversational and behavioral norms. Thus, we tend to suppress emotions when working with others.[122] We also respect personal space, do not interrupt speakers, and so on. But good manners do not constitute dignifying. Taken to an extreme, the drive for more civility may actually develop denigrating tendencies by reducing spontaneity

---

[122] Stephen L. Carter, *Civility: Manners, Morals, and the Etiquette of Democracy* (Chicago: Harper Collins, 1999).

and over-controlling daily interactions, placing unnecessary demands on workers. Furthermore, it is easy to denigrate while being civil. Civility governs only the form of conversation, not the content.

Appeals to "bring back civility" in our work and family environments are laced with elitist and conservative overtones.[123] The civility debate is actually more about restoring hierarchical authority than promoting dignity on the work floor. That does not mean that civility is not an issue in the dignifying project. However, sincere civility is the product of a dignifying milieu; it does not precede dignity.

The Guarding of Dignity

When putting forward a plan to promote dignifying, it is important to formulate expectations, to set criteria of behavior, and to encourage others to participate in this plan. No significant change will occur if we forget that we gain dignity when we bestow it on others. It is, therefore, in our interests to guard the dignity of others, even in a culture that puts a high premium on individualism and self-reliance. But how can we mandate the enhancement of collective dignity without sacrificing individual liberty and self-expression? This is a sensitive question, and there are no pat answers. Everything depends upon the organizational context. Still, it is possible to develop some general ideas and advice.

Management must set examples of dignifying behavior and reward dignifying and the guarding of dignity by others. The fundamental fact of democratic dignity can be asserted and exemplified by management in many ways and on many occasions. Guarding each other's dignity means preventing denigration from occurring or correcting the effects of denigration. One of the most effective ways for management to encourage guardianship of dignity is to enact a policy of rewarding integrity, ethical behavior, and commitment to the dignity of others. Such a policy rewards employees who report incidents of denigration when:

---

[123] David K. Hart, "A Partnership in Virtue Among All Citizens: The Public Service and Civic Humanism," *Public Administration Review* 3, (1989): 101-105.

- the reporting is done with a legitimate motive;
- all direct channels of personal influence are blocked or dangerous;
- the reporting is based on reasonable evidence, without room for other interpretations;
- the problem appears to be serious and ongoing;
- the reporting has some chance of ameliorating the situation;

When such policies are implemented, there must also be a platform for handling such reports. The assigned body, whether an ad-hoc or a standing committee, must have sufficient clout to address denigration at all levels and sectors of an organization. It is nearly impossible to guard the dignity of a fellow worker if one feels threatened with retribution.

Moral Issues

Dignity within an organization rests on a foundation of morality. Those managers who hire lawyers to deal with what are actually moral issues cannot pursue dignity, because dignifying means accepting risk, trusting others, and acting in good faith.

Moral issues present opportunities for dignifying: "To bring moral knowledge (e.g., virtues) to bear in the 'real world,' the individual needs a strong sense of what is ideal in human conduct. . . . But what are the virtues that we must practice? . . . Most seem to center around concerns for *benevolence* and *justice*."[124] Dignity is a moral stance requiring managerial integrity. An organizational dignifying policy must be supported by ethical commitment. The thoughtful, serious treatment of moral issues can give great impetus to the development of dignifying behavior. In fact, moments of moral reflection are themselves expressions of human dignity and freedom within a mechanistic organizational universe.

---

[124] Robert B. Denhardt, *Public Administration: An action orientation* (Wadsworth: Belmont, 1995).

This logic leads to certain inferences:

- We need to discuss openly and clarify how management juggles the often conflicting demands of efficiency and human concerns. Workers must have confidence in the integrity of management.
- We need to make sure that everyone in the organization understands the rationality of corporate codes of conduct. For example, does management respond to anonymous letters and phone calls? If not, this may be understood as a lack of concern for underdogs who fear reprisal. If yes, it can also signal that management is open to gossip and innuendo, possibly resulting in an avalanche of anonymous complaints. (The Dutch refer to this as "management by slander.") There is a third way, where management uses a situational approach to see if a problem exists and needs corrective action. Executed skillfully, such an approach can reveal unexpected problem areas without unleashing malicious personal gossip and witch hunts.
- Whenever possible, we need to give workers a say in addressing ethical issues. Various formal modes of organizational communication can serve as ethical forums, setting a tone of integrity not only in management circles, but also throughout the organization.

Owning Space

In most organizations, workers are allowed to personalize their work space. Employees have pictures of loved ones and other personal totems and tokens on their walls and shelves. On their computers, we find pictures of their children, spouses, or pets as screen savers. Even those who cannot put their nametag on organizational real estate have found ways to stamp their identity on something. Cabbies, truck drivers, and others who use commercial vehicles put their personal marks in and on what they consider to be *their* space.

Our tendency to claim territory is a deep psychological drive that demands satisfaction. To deny a worker the right to this naming and labeling ritual is to thwart a basic human need. Most managers realize this and do not interfere, although it is often necessary to set some rules to prevent abuse. Managers, however, often do not realize that the claiming of space is a perfect moment for promoting dignity and preventing denigration. For example, not long ago, a female employee complained to her boss about the photo on a colleague's desk of the man's scantily clad fiancée. She did not address the colleague directly. In this case, the manager had an opportunity to discuss communication between the two workers and to suggest ways for the two to coexist in a respectful relationship. While we may encourage the personalizing of office space, employees should also be given to understand that cubicles are open and public, and thus bound by communal standards and taste. The task for the manager is to find a common denominator in setting procedures and norms. The dignity of the worker and her or his peers needs to be the basic principle in this consensual process.

Space in organizations is often used to establish a pecking order. Elaborate formulas ensure that floor space, number of windows, and distance to the CEO correspond to rank. The offices of those with the most power are rarely located in the backyard or the basement. Rational policy guidelines, recognizing seniority or strict functional assessment, are often complemented by a space-reward policy that keeps workers in a trite and denigrating competition for status. In the modern office buildings of corporate America, corner offices with extra windows are held out as prizes in a contest for intra-organizational status and prestige. Space can also be used as punishment, with the basement or the office next to the restroom used as preferred tools of denigration. While nobody denies management the right to allocate space, using space purely as an expression of hierarchy and favor leads to denigration of the whole workforce and unnecessarily harsh internal competition. Acknowledging the need for personal space identification and stressing functional demands in space allotment are ways of dignifying.

Modern architects have learned to design work space that acknowledges the worker as a whole person with social, psychological, and spiritual needs and well as functional roles. Industrial engineering now goes well beyond simple ergonomics and employs theories of mental health as well. When designing new space, redesigning old areas, or relocating due to growth or consolidation; when furniture becomes obsolete or new equipment needs to be installed—in these situations, management has the chance to right old wrongs by acting in accordance with the spirit of democratic dignity.

Community Expectations

To allay distrust and increase participation, any project aimed at dignifying must be carefully explained to all stakeholders, including those outside the organization. The general public has certain expectations about the way an organization should operate. There should be some "correspondence" between those expectations and any intended project.[125] When a manager decides to put dignity on the table, he or she must be aware not only of the state of employee relations, but also of the organization's image in and interactions with the community. The success of any dignifying project is greatly influenced by the interface with the community. Dignity cannot be honored within the organization and ignored outside its walls. Hence, no dignity project can be considered sincere if it does not include the effort to dignify the communities in which the organization operates, whether or not those communities are technically customers of the organization.

Degrading the Neighborhood

Some elite Eastern universities have acquired a bad name in their neighborhoods because of their reputation for exploiting local communities and disregarding the interests of the non-academic population. For example, a university in Baltimore bought several row houses on a block and gutted these houses. Within a few years, the whole block had deteriorated and the rest of the properties could be bought at deeply discounted prices and demolished for campus expansion. This pattern was repeated several times. The policy led to animosity with the predominantly black community that

[125] On correspondence theory, see Pirie, 1988.

surrounded the school. Exacerbating these problems was the fact that the university did not hire from these neighborhoods. University decisions caused an enduring rift because the neighborhood perceived an arrogant attitude on the part of the university.

Making Your Own Grass Greener

Watching the neighborhoods around its campus crumble, administrators at Jackson State University in Mississippi decided to fight back by investing in local housing stock and encouraging new businesses. The university's business school created a revolving loan fund that helps build new housing and seeds small start-up businesses.

"We only buy vacant, abandoned units," said Carolyn Nelson of the school's Home Ownership Opportunities Program. "We do not attempt to do anything within the boundaries of that neighborhood without asking the residents. We need their input, support, and direction." Where tattered houses with peeling asbestos shingles once stood, there are now attractive, renovated homes with vinyl siding. Eight-foot privacy fencing surrounds the properties, which have backyards and driveways instead of curbside parking.

Around Jackson State, the average cost for a finished house is $40,000 to $48,000. "Cost ranges for buying these units have been from $2,800 to $22,000," said Nelson. "From the sale of the properties, the funds received go into a revolving loan fund which allows us to continue to buy, rehab, and resell units. The university doesn't plan to do this permanently. We are interested in revitalizing neighborhoods to the point that private investors will be interested again."

Why is the university putting all this time and energy into the program? "There's the altruistic reason to do good, and universities also have a self-interest. If they are in a community that's in decay and is dangerous, they won't attract students," says Rodney Green, the university's director of the Center for Urban Progress. (*The Responsive Community*, Fall 1998.)

Many universities with inner-city campuses have begun to mend relations with neighborhood residents whom they must rely on for cooperation in reducing crime, gaining the support of local politicians, creating a positive environment for prospective students, and providing minority study subjects for research. However, federal mandates are sometimes met with suspicion in minority communities. Since it is the federal government that has mandated the inclusion of minorities in research and training, and not university policy, many in the community are reluctant to participate. Often, these projects awaken fears that they are merely a cover for undercover law enforcement efforts that target members of the community.

Many other types of organizations operate in an exploitive manner in the community. Within such a company, internal dignifying projects will always be hampered by a denigrating attitude toward the neighborhood in which it operates. Developers of supermarket chains, for example, often conduct endless demographic analysis when deciding where to build a new store. Yet they give far less, if any, consideration to the effects such decisions have on the community. To achieve dignity, management must attend to the wider questions of how the organization does business. To improve community relations, organizations can use the dignifying process as a clarifying mechanism to assess their own actions and public image. If universities, corporations, or other organizations wish to reach out to the community, they must relate to local people and institutions in a sincerely dignifying way.

Denigrating the Environment

When a company pollutes, it is both degrading to the environment and denigrating to the people who live nearby. Not all pollution, however, is willful denigration. A company may have inherited a bad situation that cannot be undone overnight. It may not know that it is polluting.

However, neglecting environmental regulations is denigration, as is willful dumping of waste into streams and lakes when alternatives are available. Exporting waste to other nations denigrates whole populations, while dumping refuse into the ocean and ignoring warnings from experts shows contempt for the planet. Of course, pollution is not the only form of corporate neglect. Other types of irresponsibility include failure to maintain company vehicles properly and to perform regular safety inspections of machinery and industrial processes.[126] Denigration, here, means an exclusive focus on profitability at the expense of all other humane considerations and responsibilities. When CEOs of tobacco companies maintain that smoking is not addictive and does not cause cancer, they are denigrating their own integrity and insulting the public's intelligence. After telling such self-serving lies to the public and government, how could they hope to be believed by their employees, stockholders, suppliers, or customers—or, for that matter, by their own friends and family? Unfortunately, in the United States, those in positions of wealth and power can often get away with such gross deceit because the system is based on legal rather than moral liability.

Nobody should blame polluters and other corporate miscreants for causing harm out of ignorance. But once the facts have been established, corporate decision-makers cannot escape the moral choice to dignify or to denigrate the environment. No organization can dignify its people while despoiling the environment.

Beyond Indignity

Like the gladiatorial games of ancient Rome, the auctioning of slaves, and the public execution of prisoners, some activities and organizations are emblems of indecency and degradation. Unfortunately, there are modern versions of these old inhuman spectacles where human dignity is debased for cheap thrills, and indignity becomes a commodity. The producers of bizarre "entertainments" like *Monster Truck Mud Mania* are not likely to interest themselves too deeply in the question of individual self-worth. These spectacles cater to a level of public emotion so base that the question of dignity becomes moot. The bloodthirsty audience emotion provoked by professional wrestling exhibitions or the faked brawls of *The Jerry Springer Show* blatantly dehumanize participants and public. In this world, the masochistic desire to witness self-denigration is exploited on a mass scale. Any discussion of dignity in this context becomes nothing but a sour joke, something else for cynical media moguls to exploit.

These shows thrive on indignity pushed to the point of violence. But other organizations that deal with fighting and force must think in

---

[126] A form of neglect that led to the 1984 gas leak at a Union Carbide plant that killed thousands in Bhopal, India, and innumerable other chemical and industrial accidents.

terms of protecting dignity. The army and police must be constantly aware of dignity, both within the corps as well as in interactions with the public. When unusually fierce competition plays a prominent part in an organization's functioning, such as the trading pit of the futures market in Chicago, the need for dignifying and preventing denigration is central to good management. The implications of this observation are important, because we tend to link fighting and competition. In sports, coaches and the public often suggest "killing the enemy," "driving them into the ground," and "taking no prisoners." The male urge to fight and compete is a product of both male physiology and each culture's methods of socializing boys.

In this context, then, the call for privatizing once-public services and making education and healthcare more competitive is rarely aligned with the idea of dignifying. The current call for a "patient's bill of rights" indicates that the dignity of patients is under attack, a view supported by persistent complaints about the denigrating behavior of healthcare workers and HMOs. Healthcare institutions could change the culture of indifference to, and abuse of, patients if healthcare professionals and administrators were aware of the consequences of such denigrating behavior. It is not enough to threaten employees into being pleasant and polite, as fear is a denigrating motivation, and forced pleasantness often masks real resentment. Positive, functional interaction with the public can only be reached through managerial attention to dignity.

Corporate Sponsorship

Many companies sponsor community activities or causes. For decades, Texaco has footed the bill for radio and television broadcasts of Metropolitan Opera performances. On a more modest scale, supermarkets and pharmacies often offer space and publicity for the delivery of flu shots, while local car dealers put up prizes for Lions' club lotteries. Almost all companies sponsor something; the list of examples is endless. Sponsorship is considered a good example of neighborliness, volunteerism, and what then-Vice President George Herbert Walker Bush referred to as America's "thousand points of light"—but it is not always without controversy. When a bar sponsored a youth soccer team, several parents protested this linking of youth and alcohol.

A popular variation on the theme of community involvement is group participation by workers in charity walkathons as well as local parades and festivals. This trend is global. In Rio de Janeiro, the annual festival of Carnival is no longer so much a festival of neighborhood troupes as it is a pageant of company-sponsored floats and spectacles. A brewery in Paramaribo, Suriname, sponsors an annual half-marathon. The voluntary efforts of workers, representing their companies in a positive light, can burnish an organization's image and lift team spirit. But do these extracurricular activities really dignify participants and the larger community?

A look at the organizational budgeting process provides an answer. Most companies book community sponsorship expenses under the accounting category of advertising costs. Very few organizations consider such costs as human resource expenses or charity. While the spirit of giving and self-sacrifice that such activities encourage may be dignifying, and the educational component of charitable events can help participants recognize the dignity of others, this outcome is seldom the top priority of management. Altruistic motives aside, from the perspective of a chief financial officer, supporting good causes is good marketing. Managers who are intent on internal dignifying plans should re-examine their community relations strategies to see how charitable projects can be made more effective instruments of reducing social denigration and increasing democratic dignity.

To spur dignity *within* an organization, managers must assess their organizations' *external* relationships in terms of the dignity, or the denigration, that they promote. A company's strategic planning process, its interaction with competitors and partners, its treatment of customers, clients, patients, or local residents all reflect the company's commitment to human dignity.

The road to dignifying may be circuitous, and the obstacles can be formidable, but the rewards are substantial, including a more fulfilling life for managers and employees and stronger relationships with all stakeholders—employees, customers, investors, and the community. An organization is its people; managers and the companies they represent neglect this reality at their own peril. The dignity we protect and uphold is our own. It is up to all of us to live by the principle that dignity matters.

###

References

Amicus-MSF Union. "Parliament Debates Workplace Bullying." *Health and Safety News Archive.* http://www.amicustheunion.org/main.asp?page=344> (accessed March 16, 2005).

Antonovsky, Aaron. *Health, Stress, and Coping.* San Francisco: Jossey-Bass Publishers, 1979.

Barnard, Chester. *The Functions of the Executive.* London: Oxford University Press, 1956.

Bedian, Arthur G. and Achilles A. Armenakis. "The Cesspool Syndrome: How dreck floats to top of declining organizations." *The Academy of Management Executive* 12 (1998): 58-67.

Booher, Danny and Frank Forrestal. "Caterpillar is Forced to Recall Fired Unionists—UAW members ratify contract in close vote." *The Militant* 62, no. 13 (1998): http://www.themilitant.com/1998/6213/6213_1.html (accessed April 6, 2005).

Bourdieu, Pierre. *Distinction: A social critique of the judgment of taste.* Translated by Richard Nice. Cambridge: Harvard University Press, 1984.

"Building Business by Doing the Right Thing: Trio Behind Lombard-Based TUSC Follows that Route." *Chicago Tribune*, February 22, 1998.

Carter, Stephen L. *Civility: Manners, Morals, and the Etiquette of Democracy.* Chicago: Harper Collins, 1999.

Carter, Stephen L. *Reflections of an Affirmative Action Baby.* New York: Basic Books, 1991.

"Cat Workers Fighting Example," *The Militant* 62, no. 13 (1998): <http://www.themilitant.com/1998/6213/6213_6.html> (accessed April 5, 2005).

Chappell, Duncan and Vittorio Di Martino. *Violence at Work.* Geneva: ILO Publications, 1998.

Coates, James. "World Wide Wastrels: We Know You've Got Mail." *Chicago Tribune*, May 25, 1998.

Dean Jr., James W., Brandes, Pamela, and Ravi Dharwadkar. "Organizational Cynicism." *Academy of Management Review* 23, no. 2 (1998): 341-352.

DeCenzo, David A. and Stephen P. Robbins. *Human Resource Management.* New York: Wiley, 1996.

Deetz, S. "Critical Interpretive Research in Organizational Communication." *Western Journal of Speech Communication* 46 (1982): 131-49.

Denhardt, Robert B. *Public Administration: An action orientation.* Wadsworth: Belmont, 1995.

Department of Defense, United States Government Printing Office. *The Armed Forces Officer.* 1950.

DePree, Max. *Leadership is an Art.* New York: Dell Publishing, 1989.

Downs, Anthony. *Inside Bureaucracy.* Chicago: Waveland Press, 1966.

Essed, Philomena. *Understanding Everyday Racism: An Interdisciplinary Theory.* Newbury Park, CA: Sage Publications, 1991.

Fisher, Robert W. "The future of energy." *The Futurist* 31, September-October 1997, p. 43.

Flannery, Raymond B. *Violence in the Workplace.* New York: Crossroad Publishers, 1995.

Folger, Robert and Daniel P. Skarlicki. "When Tough Times make for Tough Bosses: Managerial Distancing as a Function of Layoff Blame." *Academy of Management Journal* 48, no. 1 (1998): 79-87.

Fox, Alan. *A Sociology of Work in Industry.* London: Collier MacMillan Ltd., 1971.

Frankenberg, Ruth. *White Women, Race Matters: The social construction of whiteness.* Minneapolis: University of Minnesota Press, 1994.

French, Peter A. *Responsibility Matters* (Kansas: University Press of Kansas, 1994).

Gaines, Sallie L. "Results often don't justify CEO pay." *Chicago Tribune*, April 10, 1998.

Garson, Barbara. *The Electronic Sweatshop: How computers are transforming the office of the future into the factory of the past.* New York: Penguin USA, 1989.

Gerth, Hans H. and C. Wright Mills. *From Max Weber: Essays in Sociology.* London: Routledge and Kegan Paul Ltd., 1948.

Giddens, Anthony. *Modernity and Self-identity: Self and society in the late modern age.* Stanford: Stanford University Press, 1991.

Gudykunst, W. B. *Bridging Differences: Effective Intergroup Communication.* Newbury Park: Sage Publications, 1991.

Hamner, W. Clay and Ellen Hamner. "Behavior Modification on the Bottom Line." *Organizational Dynamics* 4, no. 4 (1976): 2-21.

Handy, Charles. *The Age of Paradox.* Boston: Harvard Business School Press, 1994.

Hart, David K. "A Partnership in Virtue Among All Citizens: The Public Service and Civic Humanism." *Public Administration Review* 3, (1989): 101-105.

Heckscher, Charles and Anne Donnellon, eds. *Post-bureaucratic organization: New perspectives on organizational change.* Thousand Oaks: Sage Publications, 1994.

Hymowitz, Carol. "IN THE LEAD: Does Rank Have Too Much Privilege? – Special Deals for Top Executives, While Underlings Lose Jobs and Savings, Are All Too Common." *The Wall Street Journal*, February 26, 2002.

Janis, Irving. *Groupthink: Psychological studies of policy decisions and fiascoes.* Boston: Houghton Mifflin, 1982.

Kannell, Michael E. "AT & T chief defends cutbacks, blasts media." *The Atlanta Journal and Constitution*, February 28, 1996.

Kavathatzopoulos, Iordanis. "Kohlberg and Piaget: Differences and similarities." *Journal of Moral Education* 20, no.1 (1991): 47-54.

Kerch, Steve. "By any measure, office is where you live during work." Chicago Tribune, February 26, 1998.

Kiel, L. Douglas. *Managing Chaos and Complexity in Government: A new paradigm for managing change, innovation, and organizational renewal.* San Francisco: Jossey-Bass Publishers, 1994.

Klamen, Debra L., Grossman, Linda S., and David Kopacz. "Posttraumatic Stress Disorder Symptoms in Residents Physicians Related to Their Internship." *Academic Psychiatry* 19, no.3 (1995): 142-49.

Koontz, Harold, O'Donnell, Cyril, and Heinz Weihrich. *Essentials of Management.* New York: McGraw-Hill, 1982.

Leavitt, Paul. "N.C. plan owner gets 20 years in fire deaths." *USA Today*, September 15, 1992, p. 3A.

Leder, Drew. "A Tale of Two Bodies: The Cartesian Corpse and the Lived Body." *In The Body in Medical Thought and Practice*, edited by Drew Leder. Dortrecht: Kluwer Academic Publishers, 1992.

Linder, Marc and Ingrid Nygaard. *Void Where Prohibited: Rest breaks and the right to urinate on company time.* Ithaca: ILR Press Cornell University, 1998.

Mangan, Katherine. "Outrage and a Sense of Betrayal at Allegheny U. of Health Sciences." *Chronicle of Higher Education*, September 18, 1998, p. A 49.

Manier, Jeremy and William Recktenwald. "Hospital changes policy after death of 15-year-old boy only steps from the emergency room." *Chicago Tribune*, May 18, 1998.

Marsden, R. and B. Townley. "The Owl of Minerva: Reflections on Theory in Practice."

In *Handbook of Organization Studies*, edited by S. R. Clegg, C. Hardy and W.R. Nord, 659-675. London: Sage Publications, 1996.

Mayfield, Mark. "In N.C., lingering pain, anger: Fatal fire fixed in memories." *USA Today*, March 11, 1992, p. 5A.

Memmott, Carol. "Author offers ugly account of Texaco lawsuit." *USA Today*, April 3, 1998, p. 6B.

Merelman, Richard M. "On Legitimalaise in the United States: A Weberian Analysis." *The Sociological Quarterly* 39 (1998): 351-368.

Merlo, Catherine. "The triumph of Dawson's textile workers." *Rural Cooperatives* 65, March/April 1998, p. 12-16.

Merton, Robert K. "Notes on Problem Finding in Sociology." In *Sociology Today*, eds. Merton, et al., xv-xvi. New York: Basic Books Inc., 1959.

Miller, Delbert C. and William H. Form. *Industrial Sociology: An introduction to the sociology of work.* New York: Harper & Brothers, 1951.

Mizrahi, Terry. *Getting Rid of Patients: Contradictions in the socialization of physicians.* New Brunswick, NJ: Rutgers University Press, 1986.

Mooney, James D. and Alan C. Reilly. *The Principles of Organization.* New York: Harper & Bros., 1939.

Morris, Naomi. "Respect: Its meaning and measurement as an element of patient care." *Journal of Public Health Policy* 18 (1997):133-154.

Moss Kanter, Rosabeth. *Rosabeth Moss Kanter on the Frontiers of Management.* Boston: Harvard Business School Press, 1997.

Murray, Jerome. "Coping with Stress." <http://www.betteryou.com/coping.htm> (accessed March 1, 2005).

New York Times News Service, "Canada Apologizes to Aboriginal People," *Chicago Tribune*, January 8, 1998.

Noer, David M. *Breaking Free: A prescription for personal and organizational change.* San Francisco: Jossey-Bass, 1996.

Nussbaum, Martha C. *The Fragility of Goodness: Luck and Ethics in Greek Tragedy and Philosophy.* London: Cambridge University Press, 1986.

Occupational Safety & Health Administration (OSHA). "Workplace Violence Awareness and Prevention: Facts and Information." http://www.osha.gov/workplace_violence/wrkplaceViolence.PartI.html (accessed April 6, 2005).

Peters, T. J. and R. H. Waterman, Jr. *In Search of Excellence: Lessons from America's Best-Run Companies.* New York: Harper & Row, 1982.

Pirie, Marion. "Women and the Illness Role: Rethinking Feminist Theory." *La Revue Canadienne de Sociologie et D'Anthropologie/ The Canadian Review of Sociology & Anthropology* 25, no. 4 (1988): 628-48.

Pfeffer, Jeffrey. *The Human Equation: Building profits by putting people first.* Cambridge: Harvard Business School Press, 1998.

Prochaska, J.O. & C.C. DiClemente. "Transtheoretical therapy: Toward a more integrative model of change." *Pscychotherapy: theory, research and practice* 19, (1982): 276-288.

Roberts, Bari-Ellen and Jack E. White. *Roberts vs. Texaco: A True Story of Race and Corporate America.* New York: Avon Books, 1998.

Schor, Juliet B. *The Overworked American: The unexpected decline of leisure.* New York: Basic Books, 1992.

Seligman, Adam B. *The Problem of Trust.* New Haven: Princeton University Press, 1997.

Smith, Adam. *Wealth of Nations.* New York: The Modern Library, 1937.

Standish, David. "The Age of Mean: It's Terrible Out There, But is it Worse Than Ever?" *Chicago Tribune*, June 22, 1997, p.12.

Sweeney, J. and K. Nussbaum, eds. "Health and Safety, Dignity and Autonomy on the Job." In *Solutions for the New Work Force: Policies For a New Social Contract,* 153-173. Washington, D.C.: Seven Locks Press, 1989.

Sygnatur, Eric F. and Guy A. Toscano. "Work-related Homicides: The Facts." In *Compensation and Working Conditions.* U.S. Department of Labor, Bureau of Labor Statistics, Census of Fatal Occupational Injuries, 2000.

Taylor, Frederick Winslow. *The Principles of Scientific Management.* New York: Harper, 1911.

Terkel, Studs. *Working: People Talk About What They Do All Day and How They Feel About What They Do.* New York: Pantheon Books, 1974.

Toffler, Alvin. *Powershift: Knowledge, Wealth and Violence at the Edge of the 21st Century.* New York: Bantam Books, 1990.

Trade Union Council Website. <http://www.tuc.org.uk/> (accessed March 4, 2005).

UK National Work-Stress Network. "The Costs of Work Related Stress." <http://www.workstress.net/costs.htm> (accessed March 4, 2005).

van Dijk, Teun A. *Elite Discourse and Racism*. Newbury Park, CA: Sage Publications, 1993.

Vickers, Geoffrey. *The Art of Judgment: A study of policy making.* London: Chapman and Hall Ltd., 1995.

Weber, James. "Managers' Moral Reasoning: Assessing their responses to three moral dilemmas." *Human Relations* 43, no. 7 (1990): 687-702.

Whyte, William H. *The Organization of Man.* Garden City, NY: Simon and Schuster, Inc., 1956.

Wilke, John R. "Business as War: 'Corporate Misfits' Who Run Cabletron Play a Rough Game – They Exhort Staff to Battle, Fire Freely, Go All-Out To Please the Customer – No Chairs in Meeting Rooms." *The Wall Street Journal*, April 9, 1993.

Willmott, Hugh "When Strength is Ignorance, Slavery is Freedom: Managing Culture in Modern Organizations." *Journal of Management Studies* 30, no. 4 (1993): 515-52.

"Wisconsin Men Charged in Asbestos Removal." *The New York Times*, April 25, 1998, p. A16.

Wright, Lesley and Marti D. Smye. *Corporate Abuse: How "lean and mean" robs people and profits.* New York: MacMillan Publishing Company, 1996.

Made in the USA